Profitable Strategies for Sourcing and Selling Vintage Toys

Ainsleyx V. Livingston

All rights reserved. Copyright © 2023 Ainsleyx V. Livingston

Funny helpful tips:

Cultivate a sense of purpose; it provides direction and motivation.

Rotate between books that challenge and comfort; while some stimulate growth, others offer solace.

Profitable Strategies for Sourcing and Selling Vintage Toys : Unlock the Secrets to Maximize Profits with Vintage Toys: Top Strategies for Sourcing and Selling

Life advices:

Seek couples therapy if needed; professional guidance can offer valuable insights.

Life is a journey of self-discovery; embrace each phase with curiosity and openness.

Introduction

Welcome to this book, your comprehensive resource for navigating the exciting world of buying and selling Tonka trucks for profit. If you have a passion for vintage toys and a desire to turn that passion into a lucrative venture, this guide is your ticket to success.

We'll begin with a detailed Tonka Market Overview and General Pricing Guidelines, providing you with valuable insights into the current market trends and pricing strategies. Armed with this knowledge, you'll be ready to make informed buying decisions.

Buying Tonka trucks is an art, and we'll share expert Buying Strategies to help you source the best deals and build a valuable collection. Whether you prefer buying online or offline, we've got you covered with tips and tricks for both avenues.

As a Tonka reseller, one question that often arises is whether patina is valuable. We'll explore the significance of patina in determining the worth of your trucks and provide guidance on handling such situations.

The condition of your Tonka trucks can significantly impact their value. In "Should You Paint and Restore the Trucks," we'll discuss the pros and cons of painting and restoration, helping you make the right choices for your collection.

For resellers looking to maximize the appeal of their Tonka trucks, "Polishing Pays" explains the importance of presentation and how professional polishing can elevate their value.

Parting out Tonka trucks is another strategy that some resellers swear by. In "Parting Trucks Out," we'll delve into the process and how it can lead to increased profits.

Moving forward, we'll dive into the finer points of building a successful Tonka reselling business. From Brand Creation to Design, Trade-Craft, Photography, and Copywriting, we'll equip you with the skills needed to attract buyers and stand out in the market.

Understanding the dynamics of rival vs. non-rival goods, and the principles of Popularity, Novelty, and Scarcity will help you create a strategy that drives demand and enhances the perceived value of your Tonka trucks.

Reputation and the power of word-of-mouth cannot be underestimated. We'll explore how cultivating a positive reputation can work wonders for your reselling business.

When it comes to selling Tonka trucks, "Giant Crowds" can be your best friend. We'll reveal strategies for tapping into large audiences and reaching potential buyers.

As a Tonka reseller, assessing the value of your trucks accurately is crucial. In "Assessment Guide," we'll provide a comprehensive checklist to ensure you never miss a beat.

Finally, we'll conclude with a "Success Checklist," summarizing all the essential points covered in this guide, allowing you to keep track of your progress as you embark on your Tonka reselling journey.

Get ready to turn your love for Tonka trucks into a lucrative and rewarding venture. Let this guide be your companion in your quest for Tonka profit!

Contents

Tonka Market Overview And General Pricing Guidelines 1
Buying Strategies 8
Buying Tonkas Online 13
Buying Tonkas Offline 22
Is Patina Valuable? 30
Should You Paint And Restore The Trucks? 33
Polishing Pays 37
Parting Trucks Out 41
Let Me Show You How 47
Conclusion 49
Bonus: eBay Auction Power 50
Factor One: Brand Creation 60
Factor Two: Design 67
Factor Three: Trade-Craft 70
Factor Four: Photography 73
   Factor Five: Copywriting 78
Factor Six: Rival Vs. Non-Rival Goods 87
Factor Seven: Popularity, Novelty, Scarcity 99
   Factor Eight: Reputation 102
   Factor Nine: Giant Crowds 109
   Appendix A: Assessment Guide 114
   Appendix B: Success Checklist 118

Tonka Market Overview And General Pricing Guidelines

Tonka Trucks have long-term value as a highly sought after collectible. So if you are frequently at garage sales, thrift stores, or browsing the online ecommerce sites like Craigslist and eBay, then you've got an opportunity to make some extra cash.

My goal in this guide is to give you an overview of the opportunity to be had and maybe even a little inspiration too.

The story of Tonka is pretty simple. Mound Metalworks in Mound Minnesota first created Tonka trucks in 1947.

In 1955 Mound Metalwork changed it's name to Tonka Toys Incorporated. In 1964 they introduced their Mighty Dump Truck, which began the era of their Mighty Tonka line of products. Hasbro purchased the Tonka in 1991.

What Are Tonkas Worth?

Let me outline a general rule of thumb so you understand the relative pricing of Tonkas, and then I'll explain how to get very detailed pricing information.

Early Tonka Prices: Tonkas from the 1940's to 1960's are the most valuable. In general pricing frequently can run in the hundreds of dollars. So if you spot an early Tonka and can get it inexpensively, be sure to buy it.

Later Model Tonka Prices: Tonkas from the 1970's onward are very common. As of this writing they frequently sell in the $20 to $40 range in good condition. In poor condition they are worth very little.

Of course the Mighty Tonkas that were made in the early years have a higher value.

Pricing Guides To Add To Your Library

If you're going to gamble on higher priced Tonkas or similar pressed steel toys, with the goal of reselling them for a profit, then I recommend you invest in a few guides that will help you with your research.

O'Briens Collecting Toy Cars and Trucks, Edited by Karen Obrien. In my opinion the best complete guide to pressed Steel toys, it is very useful in this endeavor.

Collectors Guide to Tonka Trucks 1947-1963 by Don & Barb DeSale. This is also a good guide, however the prices quoted in the books are outdated.

So how do you find real-time prices so you don't get stuck with a serious purchasing mistake, or sell your items too low? You've got several options.

The Buddy L Museum Tool: Here is a side-note for those of you who are going to look into Buddy L trucks and other pressed steel toys. The Buddy L museum will appraise a toy truck for you by just sending them a picture of the truck you have and they shortly come back with a price. Of course this takes longer than we ideally want. Visit them at http://www.buddylmuseum.com

The Best Dynamic Pricing Tool

I like to use the phrase "dynamic prices" to refer to the idea that prices are frequently going up (or down) depending on the whims and wishes of the collector community.

This happens a lot, which means you can't depend on old information to make your buying and selling decisions. You have to keep track of what the market is doing.

To get a dynamic price for a specific Tonka item, we simply need to thank Al Gore for inventing the Internet and go ahead and use it, (sorry, I couldn't resist).

The eBay Research Tool: eBay, in my opinion is king here. EBay is fantastic for finding out about prices for Tonkas or just about any pressed steel truck or part. It gives a good approximate worth in dynamic time.

Here are the specific research steps:

1. Go to the eBay site (you don't have to be a member to access this)
2. At the top of the screen is a search bar and to the right is the Blue Search button.
3. To the right of the blue Search button in smaller writing is the word "Advanced"
4. If you put your curser under the "Advanced" word you will find that you can click it on. (Figure 1)
5. So go ahead and click on it.

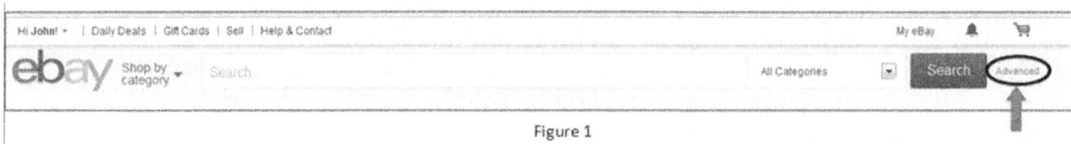

Figure 1

6. You now have access to the eBay "Advanced Search" page
7. That page should read at the top left side "eBay Advanced Search" (Figure 2.A)
8. In the next space below towards the middle you will see in a grey bar "Find Items" (Figure 2.B)

9. Underneath that is the instruction "Enter keywords or item number" (Figure 2.C)
10. In the provided box type in what you are wanting to research like "Tonka Trucks" (There are numerous items sold under the Tonka brand so "Tonka Trucks" narrows it down a bit, and you can narrow it down to as small a parameter as you like). (Figure 2.D)
11. In the next section down is the Search Listings section.
12. There are three ways to search, for <u>research</u> check "Completed listings" (Figure 2.E)
13. Now click the Blue "Search" button (Figure 2.F)

Figure 2

14. What you set in your parameters should now show up on the screen.
15. Any item that has a "Green Price" means it sold for that price (Figure 3.A) or less if it was a "Buy it Now or best offer", (see figure 3.B) where the best offer was accepted but lower than the asking price. Black price means it did NOT sell. So pay attention! (Figure 3.C)

16. Click on the item to see shipping. (Figure 3.D)

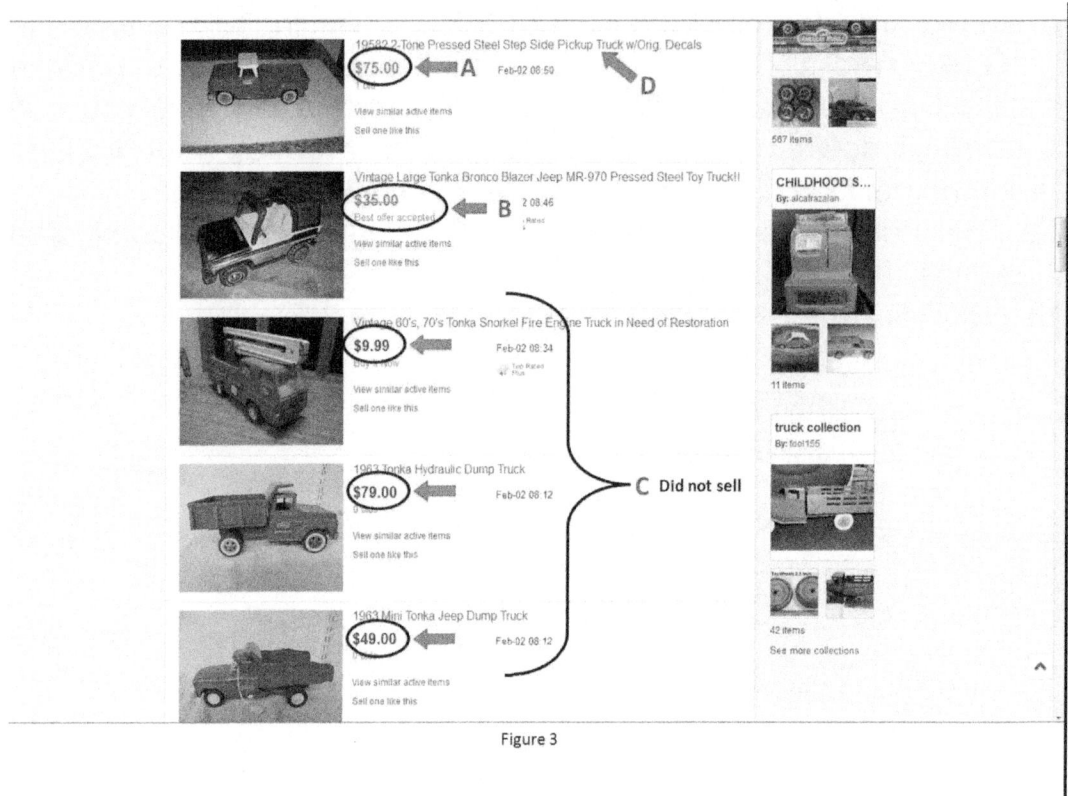

Figure 3

17. <u>Check Shipping Costs</u>. When you look at the price and it is something that you are researching you must see how much the *shipping* was. (Figure 4)

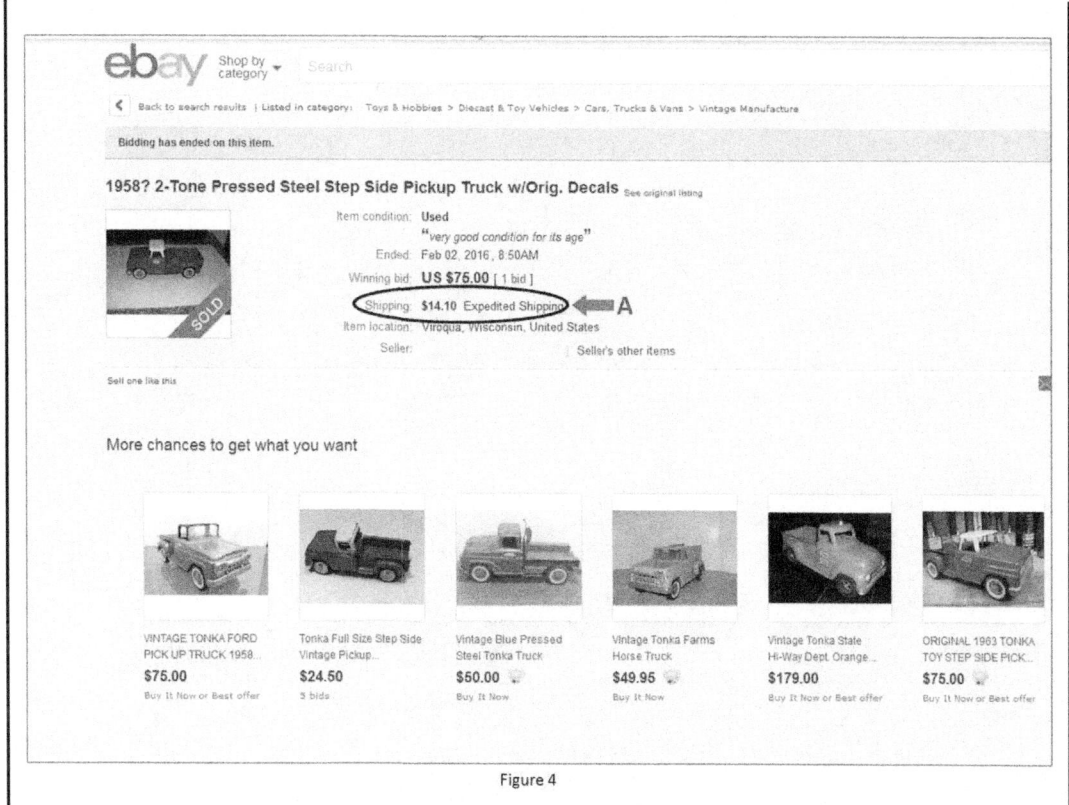

Figure 4

18. Add that amount to the purchase price to get a true number. This is important because that is the amount of money that left the buyers pocket. This is the actual dynamic price.

Learn From My Early Mistake

The reason I emphasize including the shipping costs in your calculations is because I learned the hard way it's very important.

I stumbled across a 1960's Tonka garbage truck with a starting bid of 99 cents. Here's a picture:

I won the auction for 99 cents and resold it for a nice profit, but in the process I forgot to factor in the shipping cost I had paid. When I added that expense into the equation I only made $6. Learn from my mistake and factor in shipping costs.

Chapter Summary

The Tonka market is fairly simple to understand and there are a lot of tools available to help you make good decisions. When it comes to determining prices, eBay is king.

Buying Strategies

There is an age-old saying that *"you make your money when you buy"* and it certainly applies to the Tonka market. There are incredible deals out there and it's your job to find them. In this chapter I'll outline my best suggestions for how to make that happen.

Always Be Looking

If you want to find bargains, the main principle is pretty simple. Always be looking! You can find Tonkas both online and offline. But you can't find good deals if you aren't actively looking. In the following two chapters I'll give you specific tools and tips that will help you look for vintage Tonkas.

But what do you do when you find one? I'd like to share my three big rules with you. I hope they provide some guidance as you grow your business. They are:
1. Try to spend less than $20 per item.
2. Negotiate the price as much as possible.
3. Treat people with respect and kindness.

Why Spend Less Than $20?

The Tonka market benefits from a lot of sellers who don't take the time to understand the real value of their items, so they price things way too low.

That gives you a huge opportunity to focus on finding bargains and not gambling on higher priced inventory.

By bargain, I mean spending in the vicinity of $0.00 to around $20 per item. At that price, it's hard to go wrong.

Zero? Yes, really. You'll find that once people hear about what you are doing they will just give you trucks. So don't be shy about letting people know you are buying and reselling Tonkas.

Negotiate As Much As Possible

When you pay with cash you have the opportunity to negotiate from a stronger position. I've done this a lot of times. It really does pay to have ones, fives, and tens in your pocket.

I also like to ask the sellers the question, *"what would you want for it?"* That allows them to name their ceiling and you can make them a counter offer. Many times their price is incredibly low and you can simply thank them for the opportunity and purchase the item.

Of course you should also negotiate when purchasing online. Don't assume that a "Buy It Now" price is a firm price.

Did you know you could send an email to an eBay seller offering them a lower amount on their "Buy It Now" item? On the eBay listing you simply scroll down to the question section of the listing and select "other" and make an offer and send it. The worst they can do is say "no" or make a counter offer.

How Artisan Bill Krejci's Got Started

Bill Krejci is a Charter Member of our Custom Tin Toy Trucks Artisans Guild. He got started with a single purchase on eBay. I asked him to share his journey with you in his own words.

It was Christmas of 1966 when I got my first new Tonka and in fact, it could have very possibly have been my first brand new toy that I remember ever getting.

We were so poor that if we even got toys, our parents usually got us used toys for occasions like that but we were happy with them anyway because they were always new to us!

This particular Tonka was a 1966 AA Tow jeep with the snow plow in front. I really loved that jeep and literally wore the wheels off of it playing with it! I remember tying a long piece of baler twine from my bike seat to the front of the jeep and towing it down a long gravel road as fast as I could ride with the jeep bucking and cart wheeling behind. When I got home, the jeep looked like it had been through a war zone with dents and paint chips everywhere! I think that was the end of that jeep.

Fast forward to 2004. I remember thinking about that jeep now and then and thought it would be cool to try and find one online if I could.

Someone suggested eBay and I bought my first Tonka on line in April of that year. It was missing the plow so, I bought another one that had the plow and not the tow tower and I built one good jeep out of the two.

After painting that one and putting it up on the shelf to admire, I found I was hooked and since then I have bought and sold hundreds of not only Tonka brand jeeps and trucks from 1954 to 1994, but also Wyandotte, Smith Miller, Buddy L and Nylint.

I also enjoy customizing and mixing and matching brands. I have actually made more customizing than restoring but I do enjoy doing both. It has become a great form of expression for me and is something I can do in the garage that doesn't require a lot of space!

Authors note: If you peruse the gallery section of www.CustomTinToyTrucks.com you will find plenty of Bill's work. Here's an example of a 1955 Tonka Cement Mixer that he made as a custom project. Tonka never made a Cement Mixer in 1955, which is what makes this special.

Treat People With Respect & Kindness

I feel very fortunate to have learned the Golden Rule at a young age. Christ said, *"Do unto others as you would have them do unto you and love your neighbor as you would love yourself."*

I think that principle applies to your work with Tonka flipping.

In *Lead The Field,* Earl Nightingale explains that we should learn to treat every person we come into contact with as the most important person on earth for three excellent reasons:

    1. As far as every person is concerned, they are the most important person on earth.

2. Because it's the way we ought to treat each other.

3. Because when you make people feel respected, even during a short encounter, they are more inclined to give you their business.

This applies to my work as an author as well. While some people think it's best to keep your cards close to the chest, I prefer to share the secrets, techniques, and procedures I've learned.

W. Clement Stone said,

"That which you share multiplies, that which you withhold diminishes."

These principles are paramount in my dealings with people. I trust they will be yours too.

Chapter Summary

You make your money when you buy so always be looking for bargains, never pay more than $20 for an item, negotiate as much as possible and treat people with respect.

Buying Tonkas Online

Buying Tonkas online is becoming simpler all the time. In this chapter I'll discuss online strategies and in the next chapter I'll discuss offline strategies.

Find Them On eBay: As far as eBay goes when looking for bargains I first log on to the site and I type in Tonka or Pressed steel toy truck and set the parameters for Buy it Now and Newly Listed items. If it is a good deal I snag it right then.

How eBay Helped Master Restorer Doug Bohannon

Doug is another Charter Member of the Custom Tin Toy Trucks Artisans Guild and he got started on eBay. Here's his story in his own words:

When I was just a boy I grew up living next door to a drag racer. I was infected with the high performance car bug from then on. Several years ago I was on eBay looking for a Hubley Mighty Mite jeep like the one I had when I was just a kid. To my surprise there was a whole fleet of Mighty Mite trucks.

This is where my Tin Toy Truck story begins. While spending time on eBay I came across a restored Tonka and I was like, 'WOW how cool is that.' I never knew of the 1950 and 1960 model Tonka's. I was immediately bitten by the tin toy truck bug and began buying the old rusty beat up tonkas.

My first project was a 1959 Tonka step side with custom mixed Rustoleum robin egg paint and a brass trimmed wooden bed and a custom stainless rear bumper.

My next project was turning a Tonka stake truck into a custom welder rig truck complete with custom scaled Lincoln welder, torch outfit and gas engine air compressor. I have done many trucks since then adding my own little, and sometimes large, touches.

Doug's Custom Tonka Welding Rig

eBay Tips and Tools

<u>Sniping Software:</u> If you want to get sophisticated in your auction strategy, I recommend using "Sniping" software. You put in the price you are willing to pay (don't forget shipping) and at the very last nano second it places your bid one step higher than your competition. Find one you like at: http://download.cnet.com/s/auction/

<u>Favorite Searches:</u> There are a few searches I tend to use the most on eBay to find great deals. They include:

1. The **"Buy It Now-Newly Listed"** search gives you a chance to find the new items on the site that might be a bargain. Snatch them up before anyone else sees them.

2. The **"Ending Soonest"** search gives you the chance to see what is about to end on eBay. Many times sellers who have items ending haven't gotten the result they wanted and you can get a deal. If you use Sniping Software you can set it to do your bidding for you.

3. The **"Spelling Mistake"** search is one of my favorite tactics for getting amazing deals. Some sellers make the mistake of spelling Tonka with an "a" and in their listing they type it as "Tanka". This results in them not getting any views or buyer interest because all the buyers are searching for "Tonka". In these situations you can come to the rescue and frequently get a great deal as well.

As you type in eBay use the quotation marks around the word you want to search for so eBay won't auto-correct for you. I've used the "Tanka" search lots of times to get amazing deals. Once I got a $50 Tonka garbage truck for .99 cents. Another time I got a highly sought after Tonka Jeep for .99 cents plus $12 for shipping. Here's a picture of it:

Found using the "Tanka" misspelling

Alternate spellings to look for include:

Tanks
Tamka
Tomka
Tanko
Tanca
Tamca

Find Them On Craigslist: The nice thing about Craigslist is that there is no shipping, so the price is the price. However you need to be quick on the draw. Usually the first person to call gets the deal.

Notification Tools: You can automate your searches on Craigslist by setting up a notification tool. There are lots of ways to do this depending on whether you use a PC or MAC and depending on which Internet browser you prefer. Search on Google for a few minutes and you'll find a lot of helpful articles about how to get it set up.

Over $500 Worth Of Items For $115 On Craigslist

One day I saw a "lot" of Tonkas on Craigslist. I used the dynamic pricing research method outlined previously. I used steps 1-17, there is no shipping on Craigslist, so no need for step #18).

I wasn't very quick on the draw on this deal. I saw the ad for a few weeks but didn't respond. But when a saw the price drop to $85 it prompted me to do the research on eBay to find the dynamic price of each item.

I simply printed out the Craigslist ad and looked up every piece that I could. I wrote the price on each toy in the picture as I found the item.

Low and behold just one of the bulldozers had just sold for $90. Just one of the items in the lot would make the purchase well worth it.

It was after 9pm on Friday evening when I made this discovery, so at 8am the next morning I called and sadly the guy said they just sold and the person was on the way over to pick them up.

I was dejected, why had I waited so long to research this I would have gladly paid for them when they were at $125! I ranted to my wife for the next 45 minutes. Then the phone rings and it was the guy. (Thank goodness for caller ID).

The buyer had bowed out and he asked if I was still interested. Of course I was interested!

But he threw in a caveat the price was $100 and included a wooden Tonka that he also wanted to get rid of. I was at his home within ½ hour with cash in hand.

This guy was no dummy he and his father had been collecting them for years and he knew, as well as I did, that one of the bulldozers was worth close to $100.

In the process I noticed that he had two Tonka Collectors Guide's. I asked if he would throw one of those in with the deal to which he replied, *"No those go with this other Tonka Lot for $15"*. The second lot included two collectors guides and several "Matchbox" size Tonka trucks still new in original packaging. Of course, I bought it all. So here is what I got for $115:

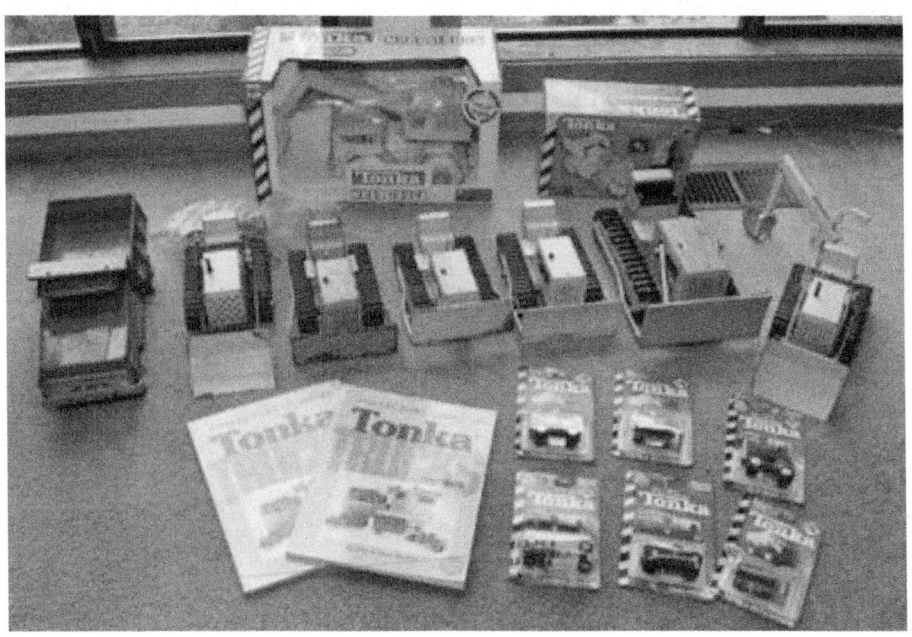

$500 plus worth of Tonka for $115

Here the kicker: the two collector guides and six Matchbox Tonkas in the front of the picture were what I picked up for the extra $15. When I got home I checked out the price of the Tonka Guide on Amazon and it was selling for $150. Wow!

So I sold the guide that was in mint condition and kept the other one for myself.

Find Them On OfferUp: OfferUp is a relatively new selling tool that is becoming very popular. It's like a visual based version of Craigslist designed for local buying and selling. It's primarily a phone based App tool, but you can also visit www.offerup.com and search there. The nice part about OfferUp is that people expect you to make an offer. So negotiating is expected.

Find Them On Etsy: Etsy is probably the second best source of vintage trucks online, after eBay. With Etsy to find the bargains you have to scroll page by page to see what you can find. To make this easier you can set your parameters for "Most Recent" and just keep track of the new items. In my experience Etsy has many inexperienced Tonka sellers and you can frequently find great deals.

Of course you can negotiate on Etsy too. If you find something you like and want to get a better price you just shoot the owner an email and ask for a better price. As with eBay, don't forget to include the cost of shipping in your purchase price.

Find Them On Less Popular Sites: Of course there are many online sites that might work well. Some that I'd suggest you look into include:

www.shopgoodwill.com
www.rubylane.com
www.ebid.com
www.bonanza.com

Buy them in "Lots" and Sell Them Individually: Another strategy that can apply to any online site is to simply purchase a set of trucks in a "lot" or batch, and then sell them individually. Many times you'll find one truck makes the entire deal worth it.

How Joe Bierbower Got Started

Joe Bierbower is another Charter Member of the Custom Tin Toy Trucks Artisans Guild. I love the story of how he got started with one very large purchase. I think it illustrates the buying strategies pretty well. I asked him to share it with you in his own words.

I've loved Tonkas since I was little. My mighty Tonka survived my three kids. I still had my original mighty Tonka dump truck bought new for me at Christmas in 1973.

I kept it stored for Years, after my kids out grew them. My plan was to restore it for my son but he tragically passed away at 19. Feeling lost for a year, I found the truck and decided to restore it for my grandson. That was my first introduction to renewing my love for Tonkas.

I needed a cab for my dump truck and answered a Craigslist add for Tonka parts for sale. I arrived in the country outside Salem, Oregon and was shocked to find he had hundreds of Tonkas complete and In pieces spread around his acreage.

Long story short, a 100-dollar bill and two full size pickup bed loads full of Tonkas and my restoration of Tonkas started. I have now been restoring and customizing Tonkas (and a few other brands) for almost 5 years.

Here is just part of Joe's $100 Purchase in the back of his pickup truck:

Joe's Truck Load Of Tonkas

Chapter Summary

Learning to use online sites and tools is a huge advantage when it comes to finding Tonkas. If you don't know how to use these tools, don't worry, just visit me at www.tonkaprofit.com and in the resource section I have a nice collection of recommendations for courses on how to use eBay, Etsy, Craigslist and more.

Buying Tonkas Offline

There are many people trying to sell their vintage Tonkas that aren't Internet savvy. They use traditional selling methods to try and find a buyer. In this chapter I'll share my tips and tricks for finding these types of offline deals.

Find Them At Garage Sales: Garage Sales are a terrific place to find deals when you know what you're looking for and have a way to quickly do research.

Here's my best timesaving suggestion. Focus your attention on the older areas of your town. Or if it fits your situation, drive to nearby towns where the houses are from the 50's or earlier.

You will find the older Tonka's and vintage toys in these communities. In my case, here in Portland Oregon, it's the east side of town. These people are from an era of keepers and their grown children many times have no interest in the toys.

My Empty Wallet Blessing

The first Sunday of the month where I worship we hold communion after which the congregation gets to contribute a special offering on the way out the door. The money goes to help those in need through our benevolence fund.

I have a personal commitment between me and the Lord to give whatever cash I have in my wallet on those Sundays.

So one communion Sunday the time came to give to the benevolence fund and I realized earlier that week I had done some handyman work and all the money was still in my wallet. It was full! An actual shiver went through me when I realized the amount of cash in my wallet. However I had made a commitment so the wad of money went into the plate. I also realized I was blessed enough to be able to go to the ATM machine and get more cash as needed.

That afternoon I stopped by a Garage Sale and asked if they had any Tonkas. The answer was *"no."* However, there was a couple standing next to me when I asked and they said that they had just been at a garage sale a couple miles away that had a whole garbage can full of Tonkas.

I drove over and sure enough there was a garbage can full of Tonkas.

They were 20 to 25 years old, not the 45 to 60 year old types I was looking for. So I asked how much for the whole garbage can. The Man said, *"Well what would you offer?"* I said *"five dollars"*, and he looked at me for a moment and said *"How about ten"*.

I said, *"Deal, but I have to go to the ATM to get the money"*. Done deal.

Here is a picture of my $10 purchase:

All This For $10

Right away I cut the smoke stacks out of the second top left truck and sold for them for $10.

If you notice the bulldozer in the top left hand corner of the picture. I eventually customized it into this logging bulldozer and sold it for $300.

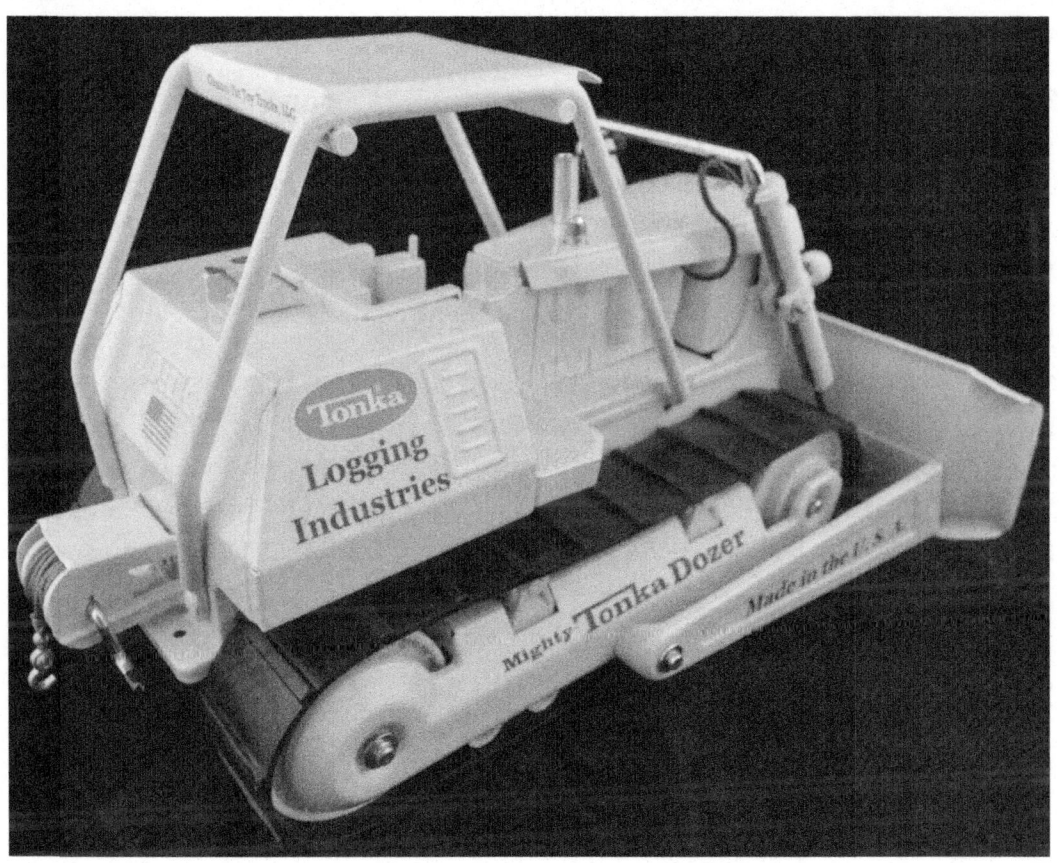

Customized Mighty Tonka Dozer

Find Them At Thrift Stores: Of course Thrift Stores are an excellent place to find deals as well. Here's one of my favorite examples.

A $10 purchase Flipped For $625

One day at a thrift store this older woman warmly greeted us. She told us that the thrift store was actually closing down. They did have a few Tonka trucks, which she showed me, but they weren't what I was looking for.

Then we went to her office and her teenage grandchildren showed me a vintage 6-inch cast iron toy car from a world's fair in the 1930's. I was excited and tried to help her find out more about the car using my eBay experience, not for my sake but just to help her out.

In the process she mentions having a truck and asked one of the kids to go and find it, which they did. She then brought me out to another warehouse and showed it to me. I had never seen anything like it before, it was missing the rear wheels and the front ones were pretty worn out but it had this "Art Deco" style to it. Here's a picture of it:

(This is the Good Side)

She said *"how much?"* I looked at her and shrugged my shoulders and said, *"I don't know"*. To which she replied, *"how about $10"*. I agreed.

We arrived home I started to research this truck and came up empty handed and was stumped until the following evening.

I stumbled across an auction listing at Christies Auction House in New York that had sold a toy Bus with the same body and grill as mine in the vicinity of $1400.

I found out that a toy company named Steelcraft made it and the trucks designer was a guy named Viktor Schreckengost.

There is a book about Viktor and he was called *"The American DaVinci"* inventor on the same lines as Thomas Edison, very prolific!

There is a museum named after him showing his artwork inventions and creations in Detroit Michigan. I bought the book and realized that I didn't just have a pressed steel toy truck but a piece of Americana!

After a very small repair, I sold it on eBay for a total of $625. Had I known the dynamic value of the truck when I was buying it I would have paid her much more for it.

I did purchase another one of Viktor Schreckengost's Dump Truck's 3 years later for $300. But I lost money on that deal. Lesson learned, buy bargains, and be very careful speculating on higher priced items.

I know you might be thinking these deals are uncommon, but all three of the stories I've mentioned in this book so far happened in a 6 to 8 week period over one summer. These types of deals have consistently happened over and over for me. They are out there if you look.

Find Them At Vintage Toy Stores: Don't forget that many antique shops and vintage toy stores might have what you're looking for too. The owners of these shops can be a fantastic resource.

My cousin told me about a toy store that had some old toys. It was on the East side of town. I went to the store and talked to the owner, Tammie, and sure enough she was selling old toys and several old pre 1941 toy trucks.

We struck up a conversation and I told her what I did. She told me that she got lots of Tonka's and could supply me with as many as I could take. I asked her how she got so many and she said she advertized with local TV commercials for old toy trucks. That was interesting!

She explained that although she had tried many different shows it didn't really work until she started to advertize during the Perry Mason re-runs on a local channel during midday. She said that advertizing during that show was like hitting the jackpot.

When you find someone in your town like Tammie, you'll feel like you hit the Jackpot. You might end up having all the trucks you can handle. That day I spent $20 at Tammie's shop for six items. Here is what I got:

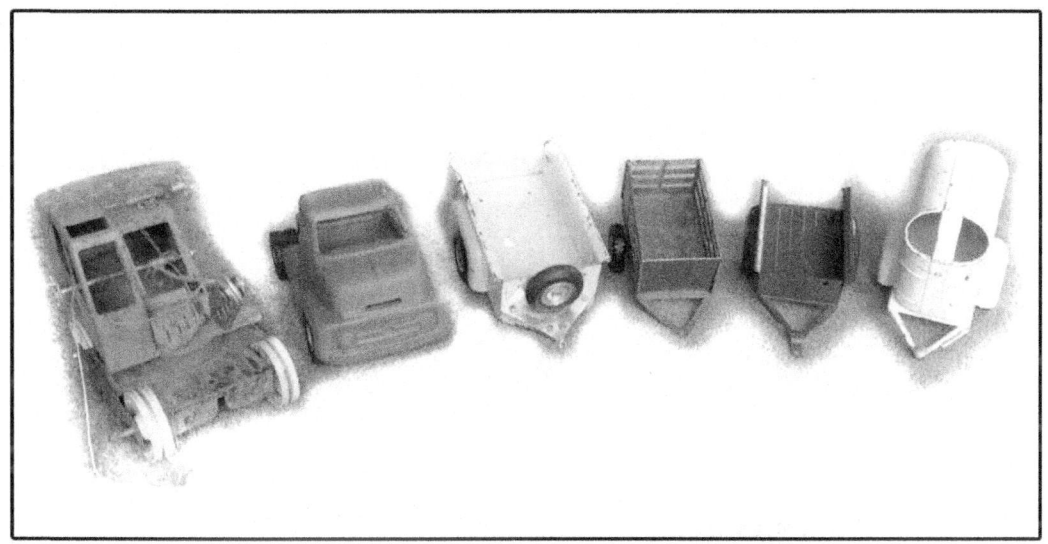

Purchased For $20 From A Vintage Toy Shop

I bought the horse trailer on the right hand side of this picture from Tammie for $2. It sells on eBay for between $30 and $50. I sold the crane on the left hand side of this picture as is for $15. I sold the tires off the yellow trailer for $19.50.

Unfortunately Tammie went out of business, so she didn't become a long-term source of trucks for me. But the experience was very interesting.

Find Them From Friends & Family: As I mentioned earlier, if you'll be bold enough to mention to your friends and family, *"I'm having a great time finding and reselling Tonka trucks"*, then you'll probably start to get free trucks.

It's A Numbers Game

In these chapters it looks as though I'm making money hand over fist. And I do make good money selling many of these toys.

But it's not always without work. It is important to mention some of these examples, such as the customized bulldozer I pulled out of the garbage can, included many hours of customization work.

Many times when I buy a lot of trucks some of them get donated to others because they just aren't worth the time and energy to list them on eBay. This happens more often than you might think.

Chapter Summary

Finding local opportunities is fun and profitable. Remember my buying rules! You make your money when you buy so always be looking for bargains. Be very careful when spending over $20 for an item, negotiate as much as possible, and treat people with respect.

Is Patina Valuable?

You basically have four options to use when trying to buy and sell Tonka (and other Steel Pressed) trucks and I'll outline them in the next few chapters. The first option is to simply leave it alone and resell it the same way you found it.

Should You Leave The Patina?

Patina is defined by the American Heritage dictionary as *"The sheen produced by age and use on any antique surface."*

Now here is the question when flipping toy trucks. Do you buy and just leave it the way it is and sell it? Faded, chipped, rust and all? In other words do you keep the original patina?

Most serious collectors would not even look at a toy truck if it has been altered in any way. The patina is what holds the value of the item in their view.

So if you run across a truck that you feel is rare, be very careful to research it before you begin doing anything to the truck. One indication of a rare truck is that it has a private label decal. Rare examples can even sell for more than $3,000 if left untouched. A few of those brands include G. Fox & Company, 7Up, Holsum Bakery, and Kroehler Furniture.

My Patina Story

One evening I looked on Craigslist and found a 1962 Tonka fleet side service pickup for $5. It was a bargain, so in the pouring rain I drove to the far side of town to pick it up.

Upon inspecting it when I got home the tires were literally rotten, the roof was bent down, no windshield, it was scratched and had mild to moderate rust. So it sat in my workshop.

The following spring we held a garage sale and I put some unwanted Tonka parts up for sale. One fellow and his friend came by and looked real close at the trucks but didn't buy anything.

A few months later he shows up asking about that ratty old truck, I quoted him $20 and he agreed. As a favor I replaced the tires with some used worn tires, straighten the roof, and put in a used scratchy windshield. I basically replaced all the parts with undesirable parts that had "patina". He went on to spend an additional $102 on more of my inventory. Here is the truck:

1962 Tonka Fleet side

I even sold his buddy a truck for $150. Patina paid off in this situation because I had other things to sell them. If you have a collection of trucks like I do, then patina can pay off.

Chapter Summary

Patina sounds good, but more frequently though, polishing pays more. I suggest you do quick flips, where you do some clean up and minor repair to the truck. It is generally more profitable. As a general rule the closer you can make the truck look to the original the better the resale value. Please realize this is not always true and if you think you have something really rare, it's wise to do some extra research before doing anything.

Should You Paint And Restore The Trucks?

Option number two in our list is the idea of painting and restoring the truck. Let's explore this option. Obviously if done correctly, it has the potential to produce the most beautiful final product, but is it worth it?

Should You Paint And Restore The Trucks?

If you were focused on profit, then I would not recommend you spend the time to do this level of work.

Painting and restoring are basically for the hobbyist. The reason it's not recommended is because when you calculate the expenses including your time, you'll most likely make very little money.

Of course there are exceptions to every rule, and I do know a restorer who can crank out the restorations and does quite well.

But any serious Tonka aficionado type collector wouldn't go near his trucks if they were aware that he uses reproduction parts that mostly come from China, like the hub caps, grills and bumpers, and on some of his work he uses reproduction Chinese frames and cabs.

Please don't get me wrong, this fellow does beautiful work, but the Chinese parts are undesirable to a serious collector.

Have I convinced you to put down the spray paint can? If you still think that paint and restoration is profitable I will tell you a story.

$9 An Hour, Really?

I got a call from an Art conservator a while back asking me to do some restorations for one of his wealthy and well know clients. I hesitated and said that "I usually don't make much money on restorations" To which he replied, *"No, you make sure you make money with this one!"*

So his client called me and I quoted the highest price I ever quoted, as a matter of fact, most of my work had never sold for what I quoted in just labor! The client paid for all the materials including the shop rags I used.

I even did some horse trading for some needed parts and made an extra $250 on the side. I kept meticulous track of my time and when all was said and done I made a little over $9 hour. I had all the tools and a complete streamlined shop to work in. That is not very impressive.

As it turns out doing complete restorations on Tonkas is similar to doing them on real cars. Most builders feel fortunate to get out of it what they paid for the parts. The labor? Ya, that's free.

Another time I was perusing eBay and I came across a Tonka Pickup that someone had restored and listed all the new parts. I added up the cost of the new parts and it was exactly what they were asking for the whole truck. The shipping was reasonable. So I bought it and I got a bunch of new parts at cost and a truck for the price of shipping. Now tell me where did he make any money? He also paid fees for selling the truck.

Again, painting and restoration is basically for the hobbyist. That's my story and I'm sticking to it.

Okay, wait, one last example:

Should We Paint This?

The total purchase price $81

A beautifully restored Ambulance

After the work was done, this nice truck sold for $200. But it took 15 hours labor, paint, and parts. The profit was about $75, but that is just $5 hour.

Chapter Summary

If you want to become a hobbyist, then you'll have a blast painting and restoring these old trucks. But don't expect to make much money doing it.

Polishing Pays

Let's look at our third option - Polishing. This one can be a very profitable strategy, so listen up. I have discovered over and over that polishing pays. So let's look at some examples.

Frequently Polishing Beats Patina

I've watched over and over as red 1954-55 Tonka Semi-Cabs get listed on eBay with "original patina". I will take the same red Tonka Semi-Cab all polished and buffed out and I will get 60 to 100% more money for it. This happens all the time. The simple fact is, polishing pays. So taking the time to learn the polishing strategies involved in getting a truck looking good is well worth your time.

$40 An Hour? Yes Please!

One day I saw an ad on Craigslist for a garage sale and it included several vintage pressed steel toy trucks. I called the gal running the show and asked if I could come purchase them early. She said, *"no you cannot buy them the night before the sale"*, but I was welcome to come by and look at what she had for sale.

I took her up on the offer and went to look over the items. I was very genuine and upon looking at the prices I could tell that she didn't know the value of what she had. I looked over all her vintage trucks and adjusted the prices for her, which was generally higher. I couldn't be at the sale the next day, but I remember telling her that she should be able to get $350 for all the trucks. She was very thankful for my assistance.

So I got in my car and started to leave and I realized that I hadn't at least try to make an offer, so as I was driving by I rolled down my window and said to her *"I'd be stupid if I didn't offer you the $350 right now"* to which she replied, *"no I will wait until the sale starts."* Well at least I tried.

Saturday comes along and in the late morning I get a call from her. She sounded very anxious and said, *"look, people have been trying to get these Tonkas for less than you said they are worth. Do you want to buy them?"*

I said, *"Sure I'll be right over"*. When I got there she said to me, *"you can have both 55 Tonka trucks for $85."* So I purchased them. It was less than what I told her to price them at, but she was just grateful that it was done. I was happy.

I started polishing. I took the Log Trailer completely apart and polished it up, made the tires and hubcaps shine, purchased some 1-inch doweling to make a load of logs and some small chain from the local hardware store.

I put it on eBay, auction style and got $127.50 for just the trailer. Next came the Red 55 Semi Cab, I took it apart and polished the painted parts and the luster came back. Then I waxed those parts, polished the chrome grill, hubcaps and shined up the tires. I put it on eBay auction and got over $140 for just the Cab.

Yes I spent about 2 hours on each of the trailer and Cab. So after paying back my investment of $85 I still made 182.50, which turned into $159 after fees. So I made close to $40 an hour and still had another cab and cattle trailer to sell.

I did the same level of work for those, but not quite as good a result, I think that set made me $130 or so.

Chapter Summary

I now do this basic polishing strategy all the time and get more bang for my buck than most of the competition. There is only one other eBayer I know of that consistently polishes his trucks and always gets top dollar like I do. I welcome you to join us.

Parting Trucks Out

You might find that you can make a nice profit by simply taking the trucks apart and selling them off on eBay. Selling Tonka parts is big business! You can sell all types of parts.

As a reminder, this works well for the pre 1970's Tonkas. Generally the Mighty Tonkas from 1983 on are much too common for this strategy to work.

How Much Are They Worth?

Prices vary widely, but the important thing to remember is that original parts are more valuable than remanufactured Chinese parts. Let's look at some examples.

In my first lot of toy trucks I purchased on eBay there was a 1960 Tonka Pumper. It was missing all the easily sellable pieces.

The rest of the truck was in great shape. It wasn't rusted or severely scratched. I thought to myself *"What a jip, a nice incomplete truck."*

This is the actual truck

A few weeks later I could not sleep so I stayed up scanning eBay. Low and behold I came across all the parts I needed.

Just a note, reproduction sheet metal parts are not painted. For that reason they are difficult to match an existing truck. The chrome parts are not as shiny or good as the ones that were made in Mound Minnesota in the first twenty-five years of production. The remanufactured parts come from China.

That night I put an eBay "watch" on all the parts and was going to think about it because they were around $80 - $100. The next morning after breakfast I went back to check in on these parts and someone had purchased them all. I was dumbfounded that buyers are willing to pay a premium price for the doors and chrome pieces.

Back then I wasn't sure what to do. Nowadays I could take this truck apart much more completely and make well over $100.

Remanufactured parts aren't cheap either. I know the main supplier of remanufactured parts. He has close to a quarter-million dollars in inventory. He wants to retire and his eBay store is down much of the time making parting out Tonkas pretty profitable.

Parting Out A Jeep Pickup Camper

A Gal I knew was having heart surgery and living with a friend, life has been rough on her and she was having a garage sale to get some money. Several times she had told me about this beige Tonka truck that she had since her childhood, just like this one:

Photo Courtesy of G.T. Kitchen

This one shown in this picture sold for a total of $14.90 recently on eBay. The one my friend had was complete like this one but had some rust. Had she sold it at the garage sale she might have gotten $8, but more likely $5.

I told her that I would take it apart and sell the parts. As a side note, a mint condition version, still in the box, sold for $69 plus shipping while I was working on this project. Here is a list of the parts I sold:

2 headlights
3 Camper windows

1 polished grill
1 windshield
1 camper door
1 camper body
1 set of four wheels
1 cab and frame

These sales took a few months. However the net proceeds, after shipping eBay and PayPal fees was real close to $95.

Now, if I had purchased the one pictured above for $14.90, and parted it out, the return on investment would have been 637.5%.

Don't Overlook The Tiny Bits

There are little wire hinge bracket on the back of the pickup and trailer style Tonka parts; it holds the bottom of the tailgate in place. Here is what it looks like:

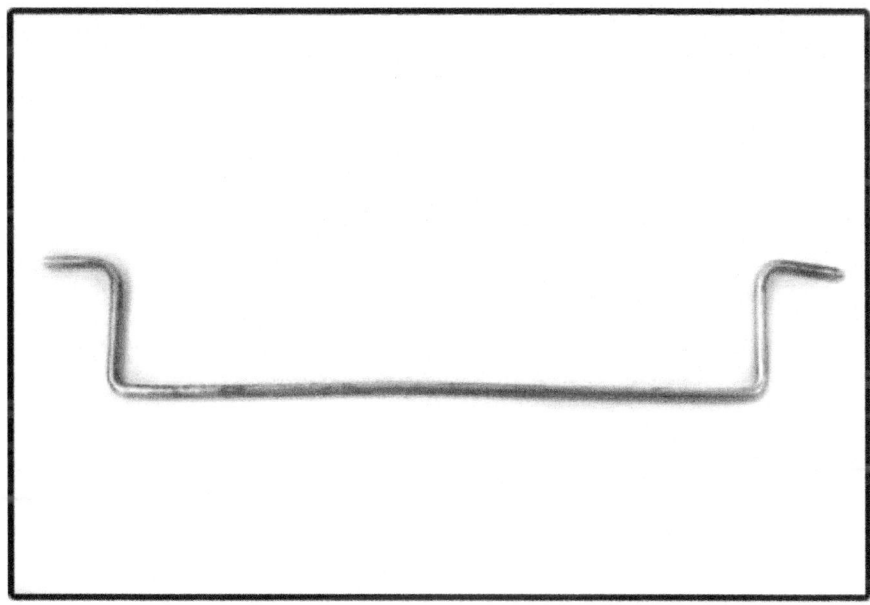

Tiny Little $7 parts

When I am restoring a Tonka truck and I don't have this tailgate hinge I use a 2-cent common large paper-clip and no one knows the difference. Here's what it looks like when it's in use. Note, in this picture there is no tailgate on the trailer:

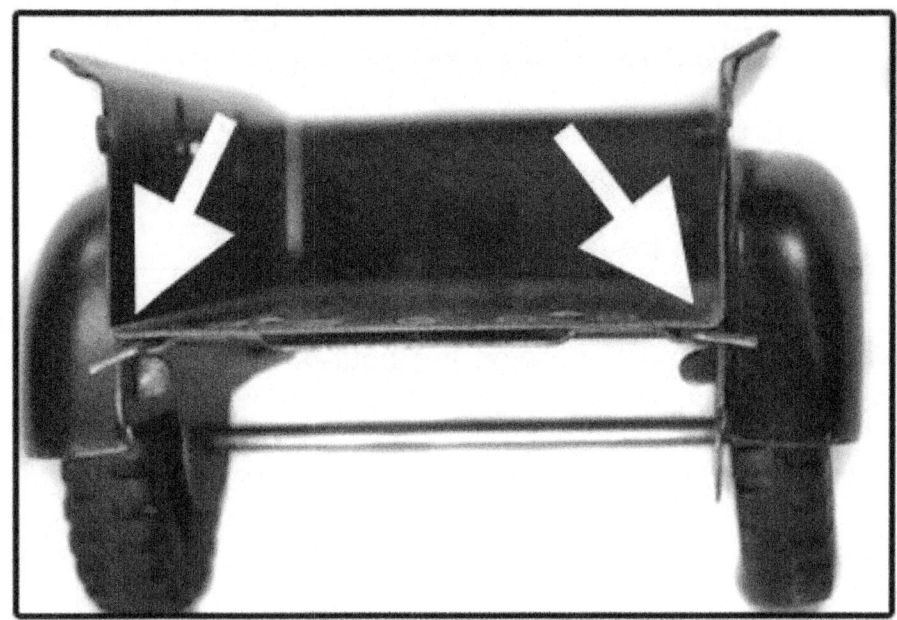

The Hinge In Pace

But the original hinge wires sell for $7 each plus $2.50 shipping. If you have them you can simply tape the hinge to some cardboard, put it in a letter envelope profit over $8.

Chapter Summary

Parting out is a great strategy for maximizing profit. I have done this constantly over the years. When selling these parts I emphasize that they are genuine Tonka parts from Mound MN USA, and not China reproduction parts. That's the primary message to communicate when you're selling them.

Let Me Show You How

If you're still reading this ebook then you must really love this topic! That's great because I do too. I'd like to invite you to join me in my workshop so I can demonstrate the techniques I use to maximize Tonka profit. So visit http://www.tonkaprofit.com today.

Unfortunately I simply can't demonstrate the tools and techniques in this ebook format, so I've made a complete video program that you can watch online. I've priced it very inexpensively so anyone that wants to get it can afford it. Again you can get it at, http://www.tonkaprofit.com

In the workshop videos I demonstrate how to quickly and easily maximize your profit. I give you the practical hands-on demonstrations that you can easily copy. I cover topics like:

- ☑ The best tools to use
- ☑ Materials that are helpful
- ☑ How to take a truck apart and put it back together
- ☑ How to make the painted parts shine
- ☑ How to make the chrome shine
- ☑ How to make the tires look great
- ☑ How to part-out a truck for profit

I know, you might be thinking you need to become an expert restorer to make money, but it's not true. Nor do you need to be a super handy guy. There are simple and quick things you can do to maximize profit.

If you're like me as soon as you see someone else demonstrate how to do something - you've got it. So I'm sure you'll benefit from watching my video course where I take a few trucks apart and clean them up. I show you exactly how to maximize profit, which is the name of the game.

Get The Free Paperback Version Of This Book: At www.tonkaprofit.com I also have a special offer for you as well. You can get the free paperback version of this book. Just cover shipping and handling and I'll send it right out.

Get The Full-Color PDF Version: We thought we'd also give you the PDF version of this ebook at www.tonkaprofit.com so that you can save it to your smartphone and use it as a quick reference guide. That way when you are at garage sales you can pull up this guide and remember the details.

Instructional Courses: I'm sure you've noticed that using Craigslist, eBay and other online sites is a key to my success. If you worry about not knowing how to use those courses, don't worry. I am constantly looking for useful courses, resources and tools for my business, and I'm eager to share those with you. Just visit me at www.tonkaprofit.com and check the resources section.

Conclusion

Buying and selling Tonkas can be very fun and profitable. I hope this guide has given you some insight into how it all works. You don't need to be an expert to achieve good results.

To sum up this entire book:

1. Always be looking for great deals.
2. You make your money when you buy.
3. There are numerous ways to make money.
4. Respect others along the way.

Most importantly there is a need for this type of work to be done, so go out there and fill the need.

All the Best,
John K. Venheim
Artisan & Founder
Custom Tin Toy Trucks, LLC

Bonus: eBay Auction Power

Because this book stresses the use of eBay, I thought it would be nice to include another bonus that focuses on how to optimize your outcome with eBay auctions.

Fortunately Jason and Cinnamon at Liberty Jane Media have previously published *eBay Auction Power* and they've agreed to include the entire ebook as a free bonus.

I hope it helps you maximize your sales outcome and gives you creative ideas related to selling your trucks via eBay auctions.

How to Use This Book:

Our system is structured as an assessment guide built around nine factors. You could call it a blueprint if you want. The assessment guide format is included at the end of the book. We've put it together so you can take the nine factors and evaluate your online auction against them. Then make improvements, and do it again. Then just rinse and repeat over and over. In that way, our assessment guide is more like an IQ test than a blueprint. You can take it now, then take it six months from now, and see how you've improved. Your ability to rate your efforts against each of these factors will give you a clear roadmap to improvement. And there is always room for improvement.

Introduction

By Cinnamon

"It's not what you look at that matters, it's what you see."

– Henry David Thoreau

It was a dark and stormy Sunday night in the winter of 2007. We huddled around the family computer in the living room of our home in Dixon California. Our goal was to list my new hand-made doll clothes outfit on eBay. As we sat there trying to figure it all out, we had different viewpoints.

- I was focused on the beauty of the eBay design templates.
- Jason was focused on writing a description that would sell.
- I was worried that my work would be rejected by not getting any bids.
- Jason was worried about how to make our new venture into a real business.
- I was wondering if people would notice that Hannah Montana (a teen celebrity) inspired my design idea - I hoped they would.
- Jason was wondering if we could make $1,000 a month doing this.

That night, sitting around the computer, our business was born. Our roles and responsibilities also took shape, and five years later, they are still pretty much the same. I focus on the design and fashion aspects. Jason does the marketing.

There was one thing we were in complete agreement on - we were both desperate for our new little venture to work. Two years earlier we had bought into the top of the California housing market, just before it started to crash. Sadly, we had signed up for one of the toxic mortgages that we shouldn't have used, and our monthly mortgage payments almost doubled.

We were desperate. Sometimes I think people say they want to start an online business, but they never do. I always think to myself - they aren't desperate enough. It was the desperation that drove us to work like crazy to make our new venture succeed. We had no other option.

Now it's a thriving business. We have five employees and another twenty contractors that work with us regularly. I would have never imagined that our small efforts would have grown so much. The concepts in this book really do work. I know starting out things seem really small. But it will grow if you don't give up.

All the best on your business efforts!
Cinnamon Miles

Introduction

By Jason

"A thing long expected takes the form of the unexpected when at last it comes."

– Mark Twain

There are three powerful reasons every artisan needs to build an online business. Let me outline them:

Internet Infancy

The Internet is in its infancy. It's a baby. It's an enormous, amazing, talented youngster. It started in 1995, with a user-group that was relatively small, but grew quickly and continues to grow at an astonishing pace. If you think the online universe is fully populated, or that all the apples have been picked, then you're really wrong. This thing is just getting started, and there is plenty of room on the bus for you and your new business. Here are three metaphors that might help you understand the magnitude of this opportunity.

A Whole New World: Imagine it is 15 years after Columbus discovered the New World. Manhattan is filled with forests, not skyscrapers. Boston has a few Indian tee-pees erected and looks more like a KOA campground than a thriving city. No one has ever set foot on Treasure Island in the Caribbean and it is waiting for someone to come and lay on its beaches. But now imagine you can travel to the New World for free, without leaving your home in England (or whichever Old World country your people originated from), without it costing you anything. You don't have to quit your job. You can go to the New World on evenings and weekends. You can find your piece of it and build your new kingdom; then, magically — with the click of a mouse — you can be back in time for dinner or to tuck your kids into bed. It's the New World, minus the risk of crossing the ocean.

Head West, Young Man: Imagine the Internet is like the "Wild West," and this is 15 years after the Lewis and Clark expedition. The Napa Valley doesn't have any vineyards yet; want to plant some? Anaheim doesn't have any orange groves, let alone Disneyland. Interested? Las Vegas is not even on the map. San Francisco? What's that? And instead of jumping on a wagon train, buying a horse, kissing your family goodbye, and leaving everything behind, you get to click into it during evenings and weekends. You can travel west, stake your claim, and work the land. Then, with the click of a mouse, be back in time to leave for work on schedule at 7:15.

Gold Rush – Internet Edition: Imagine it is 15 years after the Gold Rush started. Those nice folks at Sutter's Mill in Coloma, California saw shiny gold in the bottom of the creek, and the world changed. But you don't have to move to California or buy a physical shovel or pick. You can jump into the water; work all day picking up your gold nuggets, and return home in the blink of an eye. Get your feet wet every evening for two hours without sacrificing anythng. Bust your pick on the weekends, and never worry about getting bonked on the head by thieves or claim jumpers.

Is it really that big of an opportunity? Like the New World? Like the Wild West? Like the gold rush? It's bigger. Get the picture? This thing is big, and it's just starting out.

Internet Accessibility

The Internet has changed how business is done. Why? Because anything online, like digital products, processes, and tools, have something called "near-zero marginal cost." That means if IBM builds an amazing tool for selling something, it costs them almost nothing to add another user. They know that, and that user can be you. And there are millions of companies that are building systems, processes, and tools. So guess what happens? There is a classic "race to the bottom," where one company makes something and charges $99, then another company makes it and figures out how to charge $9.99, then a third company figures out how to make it and give it away for free to enhance another part of their business. What does that mean for you? It means people start offering you tools, processes, and products for free or nearly free. Although that might not make any sense to you, it makes sense to them and their accountants. Score.

Remember when you used to pay for America Online? Or Prodigy? What happened? Netscape came along and offered the same service for free, and figured out how to make money doing it. They "de-monetized" that product. Remember when door-to-door salesmen used to sell encyclopedias? Then Microsoft introduced Encarta on CD-ROM? Then Wikipedia started? That was an industry worth hundreds of millions of dollars a year — and it got vaporized by someone using the principles of near-zero marginal cost. That same situation is occurring over and over throughout every corner of the Internet. You are getting amazing tools offered to you, all for free. The only thing you have to do is learn to use them.

I recently heard Mark Suster, a very successful entrepreneur, share at a Stanford lecture. It was a great lecture. He explained that his first business cost him about $2 million to build, in terms of the tools and systems necessary to run it. His next business cost him just a few hundred thousand to basically build the same thing. Today, he could build the same business for just a few thousand dollars. Why? Because the tools and systems that used to cost a lot of money are now offered for free or nearly free because of this magical near-zero marginal cost.

Hey, guess what? I don't go to Stanford, and I don't live in California. I watched the lecture for free on the university's website. So let me recap the situation for you: I attended a Stanford lecture for free, listening to a guru guy talk about near-zero marginal cost. I didn't pay anything for the lecture. I didn't get on a plane and travel to Palo Alto. Stanford is happy, the guru is happy, I'm happy, and now you're happy. Was that possible 15 years ago? No way!

The online marketplace is offering you more free products than ever before and is making more money off of you than ever before. How is this possible?

I realize this will sound like I'm contradicting myself, given the fact that I just shared all about how things are getting "free." Yet there is an amazing flip side to the free coin. While things are getting free, people are spending more money online than ever before. But it's not just people spending money online, it's companies, and churches, and the government. It's commerce at the broadest level. Google is not going broke, yet it offers almost all its services for free.

Internet Scalability

All of us have experienced going from a small town to a big one and back again. It's fun to be awed by the differences. Some of us grew up in a big city and are most comfortable there; some grew up in a small town and are most comfortable there. When you're a small town kid, the big city is a weird and wonderful place.

My wife and I were small town kids in Northern California, so San Francisco was the big city for us. One year (this was pre-Internet), we were newly married, and we got into photography. So for our anniversary, we went to San Francisco to visit the camera stores and try to find a lens that we were interested in. We spent a whole day visiting all the camera stores and pawnshops. Our little town back home didn't even have one camera shop. San Francisco had more than we could visit in one day.

There were so many options, so many cool shops, and so many things to see. It was like a wild goose chase in a giant maze. We had a blast. I'll never forget driving to one pawnshop and as we got closer, we realized it was in a really rough part of town. Suddenly we realized maybe this was dangerous and we got nervous, but it made it all the more fun. We even debated whether or not we should stop and go in, but we did, and it turned out fine.

I'll never forget that shopping experience. It was with my amazing spouse, we had so much fun, and we had never indulged in a hobby to that extent before. Guess where I'm going with this story. Fast-forward a few years. Camera enthusiasts have endless options online now. The whole industry has migrated to an e-commerce existence. The options we found in San Francisco are like a drop in the ocean compared to the options we could find online today.

Something weird happens to topics and hobbies when you have a billion people online. Topics that used to be so marginal and "out there" now have huge forums and communities that you can participate in. Imagine an ant that is the size of a dinosaur. Imagine a dinosaur the size of Texas.

So the online marketplace is growing to an unfathomable size and scope — and with it, the information, products, and opportunities associated with very small topics (or niches) are growing at this rate as well. Your "thing" just got put on steroids. Your hobbyist group of four local friends just got expanded to the size of a packed out Wrigley Field. Do you know how many people want to buy a coke at Wrigley Field? A lot. So sell coke. Small things have become big, and big things have become utterly unrecognizable. If you're interested in selling, this is the arena for you.

But you've probably already figured this out if you've been online for any length of time. You searched for your hobby and had your mind blown away. It changed you forever. Great.

Now the question is simple. Can you turn that little hobby, that love affair, that passion into a profitable business? These three factors — infancy, accessibility, and scalability — all add up to one truth: You can do this!

You can do it from your home, and you can do it cheaply. The barriers have fallen, and the opportunities really do exist. It's a whole new world.

Our auction system is designed to help you learn one part of the online selling puzzle. It's not the total solution, but it is one key part. If you can consistently run successful and profitable online auctions, then you can do something that most other online sellers cannot. Having that tool in your toolbox will help you for years to come and serve as a great onramp to bigger and better selling strategies. And the cool part, the really awesome part, is that the process you have to go through to create a successful auction business will require you to lay the groundwork properly for long-term success. In other words, it's a great place to stake your claim

Factor One: Brand Creation

"My mother said to me, 'If you are a soldier, you will become a general. If you are a monk, you will become the Pope.' Instead, I was a painter, and became Picasso."

– Pablo Picasso

Legend has it that Pablo Picasso was sketching in the park when a bold woman approached him and started a conversation.

"You're Picasso, the great artist! Oh, you must sketch my portrait! I insist."

So Picasso agreed to sketch her. After studying her for a moment, he used a single pencil stroke to create her portrait. He handed the woman his work of art.

"It's perfect!" she gushed. *"You managed to capture my essence with one stroke, in one moment. Thank you! How much do I owe you?"*

"Five thousand dollars," the artist replied.

"B-b-but, what?" The woman sputtered. *"How could you want so much money for this picture? It only took you a second to draw it!"*

To which Picasso responded, *"Madame, it took me my entire life"*.

What does your brand mean to people? What does it mean to you?

A good brand is an amazing asset. A brand is obviously more than just a name, or a logo, or a slogan. A brand conveys deep meaning.

Branding is both extremely complicated and extremely simple. At the heart of the issue is one simple concept — You need a business name, image, logo, and slogan that retain your worth and symbolize the worth of your products or services.

So the secret is this: Great brands are built over time by continuously creating great products. It might only take one or two auctions to establish your brand, but it does take some time. Over time, the brand becomes so well-respected that people will bid very aggressively to have anything you produce under your brand name. In our experience, you will not get aggressive bidder action in an auction if you don't have a trusted brand.

So how exactly do you get a brand that is highly valued? In this chapter, I'll outline 10 techniques to create a successful brand.

And as a side note, if you want my #1 (by far) recommended educational book on this topic, to really go deep and learn some terrific insights, it is *Branding for Profit* by Trump University. It's an audio course taught by two brand experts. You will learn so much from it. Even if you think you know what you're doing, you'll learn more. I know, you might not be a Trump fan, but that's okay. Trust us, we've consumed lots of branding books, and his is the best. Okay, let's get down to business; here are our recommendations for brand building.

1. When choosing a potential name, consider using your own name or a unique proper name. Next, Google it to see if it has too many similar results, if any. If there are too many similar entries, keep looking. Choose something unique, then use Google to confirm it. It's not impossible. Keep trying. If you fail to do this, you'll be sorry. Wouldn't you be horrified if you picked a name and then found out later that it was already associated with something yucky, or gross, or morbid, or totally inappropriate? Or more likely, if there were 100 other companies all trying to use the same name? Bad, right?

2. Don't be cute. If you want to be taken seriously, pick a name that sounds like a real company. Pretend you have 100 employees, and they are explaining where they work to someone else. Will the name sound good in that context?

3. Avoid using the category as a default portion of your name. For example, if you use a name such as "So and So Doll Clothes," you've used two generic words in your brand name — "Doll" and "Clothes." You want to avoid generic words, because they'll never be associated with you. You cannot own them in your prospects' minds. They are associated with the concept or the category, and not with you. Not good. As a side note, lots of the mommy coupon bloggers are getting this all wrong right now. They are adding on the category words in the hope that they'll be remembered, but just the opposite happens. The entire category is growing, and some will be winners, but it will probably be the ones with the strongest brands. For example, as I'm trying to think of a blogger in that category right now, the one that comes to mind is (uniquely named) "Northern Cheapskate." No "Mommy" or "Coupon" anywhere in there. The best book about this specific issue is *Positioning: The Battle for Your Mind*, by Al Reis and Jack Trout.

4. Consider the attributes you want to convey. Choose a name that communicates attributes that are helpful to your cause, attributes that reinforce what you're trying to convey to the world. "Nike" means champion. That's cool, right? "Northern Cheapskate" makes it sound like the writers aren't from New York City or Hollywood. They must be from someplace cold, harsh, rural, and frugal. Find and build into your brand meaningful attributes that people will admire.

5. Clarify your brand attributes. What do you want people to remember about you? Boil it down. Boil it down to one word. Then try to have that word reinforced by everything you do. But here is the

critical part: The attribute must be available right now in the minds of the consumer. It can't just be what you want to become, it has to be what your customer can appreciate, recall, and attach to your brand right now. Ideally, it should be something that they want but cannot find. Liberty Jane exists as a little company in the American Girl doll space. Our word is "trendy." It's our guiding light. Brand attributes don't just say what you ARE about; they also say what you AREN'T about. If we're trendy, can we do historical outfits? Nope, not trendy enough. Al Reis' classic book, *Focus: The Future of Your Company Depends on It*, does a deep dive into this issue.

6. You can always own a niche if you go small enough. Maybe you're thinking, *but all the good attributes are taken*. Wrong. There is one simple trick you need to consider to find your attribute — think narrow and deep. In every category, (as you search on Amazon or eBay, for example), there are category leaders. But part of the power of Internet marketing is that if you want to own a single attribute and become known for it, there is almost endless open territory available for a good solid brand. The most interesting new thinking on this issue that I've found is from author and video blogger Gary Vaynerchuk in *Crush It!: Why NOW Is the Time to Cash In on Your Passion*.

7. Your biggest brand attribute is your price. New customers have an amazing sorting function in their brains that kicks in immediately, and the first filter is price. You will either be thrown into the expensive or inexpensive bucket in their minds. It doesn't matter if you don't like it; that's how it works. Companies spend millions of dollars trying to manage their way around this, or convey deeper attributes of their brand, but most successful brands are very clear about this fundamental issue. In terms of price, they've chosen to go either high or low, premium or discount. Staying in the middle is a hard place to live as a brand. If you want to go deep on this issue, the best new book is *Priceless: The Myth of Fair Value (and How to*

Take Advantage of It). And as a word of encouragement, if you're making items at home, think long and hard before choosing a low pricing structure. Our best advice is to position yourself as a premium provider. All it takes is one signature item to really pop in value for your brand to take on the attribute of being "ultra premium." We'll talk more about ways to get that first big price pop in the next few chapters. It should be your highest priority.

8. Be real. If you're going to be an exclusive artisan, then don't act bigger than you are or overly corporate. People buy from people. Your brand, after getting a high or low price tag in the minds of prospects, will get a "cool" or "uncool" tag. And the single most important element in getting a cool vote is authenticity. Be authentic. The important part to understand here is that once people see your brand and answer the high or low question, then they'll start to judge you on the merits of what you've presented, and they'll quickly make a determination about whether you're cool or uncool. In *Focus*, Al Reis and Jack Trout say that "somewhere in the corner of the prospect's brain there is a penalty box for brands they decide are losers." Don't be in that box. My favorite business book of all time, *Growing a Business* by Paul Hawken, has a great section on this. Paul Hawken is the founder of Smith & Hawken (notice the nice proper name choice). The book was written pre-Internet, but it's so solid that it's a must read for anyone interested in starting a successful business. Of course, you can still find it on Amazon even though it was published in the 80s.

9. Polish it up. These days, there is no reason you can't have a professional-looking logo. Start with your basic idea and the attributes you want, and then get it professionally polished. Try Elance if you want to hire somebody. You'd be surprised how fast, easy, and inexpensive it can be. You can also try 99designs.

10. Don't be afraid to change! This is outlined beautifully in the Trump University branding book referenced earlier. True brand equity is not tied to your name; it is tied to the deep meaning and relationship that customers have with your business. If you need to change your name because it is not effective, don't be afraid to do it. If you do it carefully and systematically so customers are along for the ride, you won't lose anything — and you'll gain a lot. There is never a reason that you have to be stuck with a poorly chosen name. Re-imagine, re-invent, re-launch.

The Deep Meaning Your Customers Desire

The goal of your brand-building efforts is to create deep meaning that you share with your customers. Don't just choose a name. Think about the deep meaning you can share with your customers.

When we were brainstorming the name for our little company, we knew that it needed to relate to American Girl in some way. We kicked around lots of names, and then realized our daughter's name fit perfectly (at least we think it does). It conveys Americana. It does that because she was born around the time of the 9/11 attacks, and we were feeling particularly patriotic back then, so we deliberately chose a name that felt "American" when we named her. Years later, we were looking for a good brand name to support the American Girl ecosystem and the stars aligned around "Liberty Jane."

But before we could claim the name as a good fit for our little business, we Googled it and the only reference we found was to an old song. So we figured we could really dominate it on Google. We were putting together the pieces of a solid brand, starting with a proper name and deep meaning. Harry Beckwith has great information on this in *Selling the Invisible: A Field Guide to Modern Marketing*. Keep thinking until you find a name that allows for deep meaning.

We've learned over time that just creating high quality outfits isn't enough to be successful. We've learned that customers are interested in deep meaning, meaningful relationships, and connecting with kindred spirits.

In his book *The E-Myth: Why Most Businesses Don't Work and What to Do About It,* Michael Gerber says:

> When you ask a business owner what they do, they instinctively respond with the name of the commodity they sell. We're in the computer business, or we're in the hot tub business — always the commodity, never the product. What's the difference? The commodity is the thing the customer walks out with in their hand. The product is what your customer feels as he walks out of your business. What he feels about your business, not what he feels about the commodity. What he feels about the experience of doing business with you. Understanding the difference between the two is what creating a great business is all about.

If Gerber is right (and we think he is), then there is another question that his idea prompts — What does the customer do with that feeling? It's simple really; she associates it with your name, logo, slogan, and work and files it all away in her memory. In short, she attaches it to your brand. Days later, when she sees your name, those feelings are attached. Or when something else prompts those feelings to come up, she thinks of your brand.

Build a brand you can be proud of for years to come. Build something that can stand the test of time. Build something that resonates with your target customer.

Factor Two: Design

"A designer knows he has achieved perfection not when there is nothing left to add, but when there is nothing left to take away."

– Antoine de Saint-Exupéry

The design of your product has a tremendous amount to do with the final auction results you'll achieve.

When we started on eBay in 2008 in the doll clothes category, we didn't know what the competition was doing, nor did we know what types of outfits would sell. My wife Cinnamon had a vision for doing doll versions of ultra-trendy outfits from stores like Forever 21 or The Limited. She wanted them to be "on-trend," as they say in fashion circles. But we didn't know whether that would sell.

What we discovered was that there were doll clothes sellers with very respected brands who did historical outfits, but not much competition in the "ultra-premium, on-trend" category. Turns out we sort of made it up, to some extent.

In a book like this, there is no way to fully cover the topic of design for all niches of the artisan world. And since we will assume that not everyone reading this is into doll clothes as their art form, it would be wrong to focus on that discipline exclusively anyway.

But for the purposes of this book, let's make it easy. If you're going to achieve amazing results financially, then you've got to meet or exceed the design skills of your competition.

In our case, with no disrespect to the market participants from 2008, it wasn't very hard to introduce designs that were more interesting, sophisticated, and visually appealing than the competition. In that regard, it seems that our eye for design and our ability to bring it into existence brought sophistication to a market that wasn't used to seeing it — again, in the ultra-premium, on-trend category.

What about your niche? Are there specific types of designs that people will pay top dollar for? In the doll clothes niche, there are two clear categories: historical clothing and contemporary clothing. Designs in either of those genres can do well.

Regardless of the type of niche you're in, there are several ways to systematically improve your design efforts. Here are just a few:

Assimilation: There are lots of directions to take this design concept. For example, you can adapt a pop culture style into your market niche. Let's say you make custom golf carts and you've noticed that "spinners" are all the rage on the custom hot rods at the car shows. Why not adapt that idea and create spinners for your next custom golf cart? Or, if you make custom watchbands and you notice Silly Bandz are all the rage with kids, why not incorporate some aspect of Silly Bandz into your next project? Get the idea? Be the assimilator of pop concepts (or any interesting concept) into your niche.

Zig when others zag: Another simple concept for design interest is to be a countercultural influence. Are other people doing designs in black and grey? How about designing in neon green? Are most designs complicated? Make it simple. Are most simple? Make it complicated. You get the idea.

Study the masters: There is more design idea documentation now than ever before. A long time ago, you needed to go to a library to study someone else's work. Now you can just read blogs, watch videos, browse magazines, and surf the net. You'll find the best and brightest in your field and other fields. Learn from them. As Tim Ferriss in *The 4-Hour Workweek* says, "Find Yoda."

Dare to make mistakes: If you don't innovate, you're not going to find interesting pockets of customer desire. Find the line, and then cross it. If customers respond positively, then you're off and running. If they don't, then look for another angle.

If you are designing products that are not resonating with your target market, but you see other sellers who are, then learn from them. Ask yourself the hard question: "Are my design skills in need of upgrading?"

Factor Three: Trade-Craft

"When love and skill work together, expect a masterpiece."

– John Ruskin

Let's face it; just like most people are average, most collector or hand crafted eBay and Etsy items are average. That's just a fact. But there is no reason you can't produce items that are way above average. Of course, few of us will ever be as good as Picasso, but we can learn from his experiences.

According to Wikipedia:

> Picasso's father, Ruiz, was a painter who specialized in naturalistic depictions of birds and other game. For most of his life Picasso's father was a professor of art at the School of Crafts and a curator of a local museum. Picasso showed a passion and a skill for drawing from an early age; according to his mother, his first words were "piz, piz", a shortening of *lápiz*, the Spanish word for 'pencil'. From the age of seven, Picasso received formal artistic training from his father in figure drawing and oil painting. Ruiz was a traditional, academic artist and instructor who believed that proper training required disciplined copying of the masters, and drawing the human body from plaster casts and live models. His son became preoccupied with art to the detriment of his classwork.
>
> On one occasion the father found his son painting over his unfinished sketch of a pigeon. Observing the precision of his son's technique, Ruiz felt that the thirteen-year-old

Picasso had surpassed him, and vowed to give up painting.

It starts with an unbiased review of your work. Is your work less impressive than others in your niche? You've got to honestly evaluate how you're doing. I love this quote by James Bennis:

> *"Don't just learn the tricks of the trade. Learn the trade."*

Your level of craftsmanship can be a huge advantage over other sellers. As we mentioned in the Auction Factor One section, your greatest brand attribute is the price you get for your items. Working to get just one auction that really pops will reposition your brand as "hot," "ultra-premium," and "highly sought-after." Obviously, those are all the descriptions you want to hear if you're expecting to get ultra-premium auction prices.

Like me, you've probably seen a million eBay or Etsy listings that start with a phrase like, "I've been sewing for 40 years." But sadly, their outfits are a disappointment. These sellers have mistaken time spent on their craft with the quality of their design and finished product. They are two different things.

In terms of creating a brand, it would be better for a novice seamstress to spend two months on one outfit than for a veteran seamstress to spend two hours. The result would be that the novice will be perceived as "an amazing new designer," whereas the veteran seamstress will go unnoticed in the marketplace.

If you feel that you need to brush up, then here are a few quick ways to boost your skills:

1. Learn the latest techniques and don't make excuses to avoid them.
2. Watch online video tutorials about "what's hot."

3. Go back and take more classes at a local community college or trade school.
4. Reinvent your design style by mixing traditional methods with contemporary ideas.
5. Enroll in our Design Academy to see how we approach doll clothing design.

Obviously, effective auctions are about design, material choices, craftsmanship, and of course selling.

So the "tradecraft" for making and selling doll clothes, for example, is a balancing act between sewing-related skills and selling skills. The tradecraft is not just about sewing. Okay, I've repeated it a couple times, but I want to repeat it one more time in the following auction tip to make sure you heard it clearly.

Auction Tip: The tradecraft we're talking about is both a product design skill set as well as a selling, marketing, and branding skill set.

But here's the good news: You are probably your toughest critic, just as we are when we evaluate our work. Lots of times artists are brutal critics of their own work, and the average person (not being informed on the tradecraft) will look at the finished product and be very impressed. So go easy.

Get other people's perspectives. Take your best shot at selling, and if the response is flat, ask yourself the hard questions about quality.

Factor Four: Photography

"It is my intention to present — through the medium of photography — intuitive observations of the natural world which may have meaning to the spectators."

– Ansel Adams

Physically touching an item is the single most important component of buying, according to shopping expert Paco Underhill, author of *Why We Buy*. When marketing goods online, your pictures and written descriptions become a proxy for the physical act of touching the item.

In some ways, it seems silly to write about picture-taking skills, because it's so commonly written about on the Internet. So we'll keep this section short. Sadly, lots of folks selling doll clothes and other handcrafted goods have decided not to focus on this important part of the presentation, and we believe that's a disastrous mistake. We believe strongly that photography is one of the most important skills a seller must learn.

Here are our top tips to quickly get up to speed on this topic:

1. Go to Google, search for "taking great pictures" or something similar, and then read 10 articles with a notepad at your side.
2. Take notes and make a collection of all your favorite ideas.
3. Take 100 pictures, trying out the various techniques. When it comes to photography, like with any other tradecraft, practice makes perfect.

Okay, those weren't really tips as much as they were tips for finding and using tips. So here are seven specific, actual tips:

1. Natural light — Go outside! The best pictures will be warmly lit, but not harshly lit. Natural light is the easiest way to get your lighting right. Obey this rule and your pictures will improve tremendously. We never use a flash, and you should avoid it, too. Our lenses allow us to operate this way (read further to find out about our equipment). Natural light with no flash is best.

2. Want a white background? A simple way to shoot on a white background and still be outside is just to use white foam core board from the art supply store. Use one piece for the ground, setting your item on it, and one piece immediately behind the item. We use our patio table for this all the time. The effect will be a fully white background shot in warm light.

3. The Golden Hour. Take your pictures an hour or so before sundown. This is well known as the absolute best light of the day, and photographers call it the "golden hour." You can shoot outside earlier if it's overcast, but if it's sunny, shoot during this specific time. There is a reason it's called the golden hour. Photos come out amazing! Glowing, warm, beautiful.

4. No clutter! More important (almost) than the item you're shooting is the background. Remove all clutter. Find a solid surface, ideally one that people won't recognize, and use it as the backdrop. Place your item four or five feet in front of the backdrop, rather than right up next to it.

5. Get closer to your item. Why do so many eBay sellers take their product, set it against the kitchen cabinets, and then back up 10 feet to take one picture and call it done? You can do better. Get close, and then get closer! You don't need to take a

picture of the entire item in every shot. Some can be extreme close-ups to show the details.

6. Crop and saturate. If you open your pictures in Windows on a PC, you can generally edit the images. Crop them so they are as tight as possible on the main object. Then saturate them, but not too much. Saturation warms up the image. Just be careful not to affect the color too much. You don't want it to be an inaccurate representation of the original product.

7. Take a lot of pictures! There is no substitute for taking a lot of pictures with your camera on slightly different settings. For any given product we are going to sell, we usually take over 100 pictures. We sort them into "good ones" and save those as a separate folder on our computer. Our folder structure ends up looking like this: "Auctions," then "Spring 2010," then "U.K. Holiday," then "Good Ones." Then we look through those for the absolute best five or six photos. We use those in the listing.

Equipment

Camera: We've used various cameras, and the one we always return to is our old 2003 Canon Digital Rebel SLR (Single Lens Reflex). Now that these cameras are common, people abbreviate all of this to say "DSLR," which simply means a full-featured digital camera that permits changeable lenses. These are the "big" cameras, in contrast to the point-and-shoot style cameras. You can buy one of these original Canons on eBay for around $100.

Lenses: DSLRs permit you to use a wide variety of lenses, including lenses that professional photographers use to get their amazing portraits. This can get a bit overwhelming and confusing, so our best advice is to find someone who knows more than you do and learn from them. If there is an old-school camera store in your town, start there. Generally, store employees can be incredibly helpful.

For our doll photography, we use a portrait lens. Used by professional photographers, these fixed-length lenses don't require any zooming in or out. A great starter lens, which we use all the time, is a 50mm f1.8. You won't find these very frequently on eBay, but you can buy them through Amazon. Generally, you can find them for $79 to $99. Another great lens, which we also use frequently, is a 85mm f1.8. This one will cost you more, and you probably don't need it unless you're a photography hobbyist.

Obviously, getting new camera gear can be a major expense, so we advocate learning as much as you can about the gear you have before you spend any money. Frequently, the newest gear is the most complicated, so if you're confused with your old simple camera, you might be twice as confused with your new fancy camera. So learn all you can with what you have and then use caution when buying. Remember - never ask a cameraman if you need a new camera.

Settings

Depth of field: The power of portrait lenses is that they allow you to create "depth of field" systematically. Depth of field is the effect that gives pictures a blurry background while the primary subject is in perfect focus. You can achieve this by shooting your picture with a low "f-stop." You can learn how to do this by watching one of the countless YouTube videos on this subject.

Image size: Our camera shoots images at 6.1 megapixels. One benefit of using a camera this old is that the images are actually usable without having to be reduced in size. It's actually very nice. If you buy a brand-new DSLR, you'll need to adjust the settings so that your images aren't 10 megapixels or more. If they are, they are almost totally unusable on the Internet without being reduced in size.

Additional Tools

Animoto. Animoto lets you turn still pictures into an interesting movie with sound and effective visuals. Best of all, it is free and very easy to use. If you export your Animoto video into YouTube, then you can embed it into your auction listings. This gives instant impact in your descriptions without any actual writing.

Photobucket. Okay, we don't really love Photobucket as a tool, but we like what it does for us. We haven't been willing to change to another photo sharing tool. Anyway, with Photobucket, you can upload pictures and then embed them in your auction listings. This makes your inclusion of lots of pictures totally free. We generally add a few pictures to our listings via eBay, and then add more in the description via Photobucket.

Learning More

Fortunately for all of us, YouTube is a terrific resource for learning how to use your camera. If you get a Canon DSLR and a portrait lens, then you'll be blown away by the photo tutorials available to you. Can't afford a new camera? No worries! Just go to YouTube and search for tips on using your own camera.

To get massive auction success, mastery of photography is just as important as mastery of your primary trade skill (be it sewing, knitting, or anything else). Don't give yourself a pass and say it isn't critical. It is.

Factor Five: Copywriting

"Either write something worth reading or do something worth writing."

– Benjamin Franklin

Writing is a critical part of effective selling. Create nice, amazing, and fun listings with your words, product names, pictures, and use of eBay templates. Draw your bidder in with this type of "digital touch."

If you do "bad touch" things, like using blinding yellow neon as your font color, don't expect your bidder to have a "good touch" experience. A good touch experience will result in comfort with your listing and enthusiasm to place a bid. A bad touch experience will result in prospects quickly leaving and never coming back.

Use Long Descriptions

So if your words and photos are a proxy for physically touching the item, then as David Ogilvy, the master of direct response marketing, makes clear, long-form copywriting clearly works better than short-form writing. You want to give shoppers as much information as they could possibly want. They've stopped, looked, and are now seriously considering buying your item, or bidding on it at least. They won't mind if you have an extra paragraph about why your fabric is better than your competitors.

Paco Underhill goes on to suggest that the single most important factor in determining whether customers are going to buy something in a physical retail environment is the length of time they stay in your store. Does this translate to the Internet selling environment? We believe it does.

You have a choice on eBay. Enter substantial details, or say a little, or say nothing. If you choose to say little or nothing, your bidders will absolutely be less comfortable than if you had added substantial facts and details. So, your wisest approach is to be sure you consider and then answer every question your buyers might have. They will read it all. The people who aren't interested won't read anything anyway, so long-form descriptions are the only sensible approach. Make it a fun and memorable digital touch.

Write for Your Audience

I consider eBay to have two types of shoppers. I realize this is a simplification of the situation, but generally it's true. They are bargain hunters and treasure hunters.

What are bargain hunters? They're people looking for a familiar commodity that they need or want. They are looking for a standardized item that they are familiar with and can easily assess the value of. They will compare your offer to everything else they see and look for the best deal. Bargain hunters make a calculated bid with the hope of getting something for less than it is actually worth. They know the common value and get interested in anything that looks like a discount.

What are treasure hunters? Treasure hunters are looking for something special. Generally, the item is one-of-a-kind (OOAK) or unique in some special way. The item is usually valuable to different people in different ways. The item is not simply assessed based on economic worth, but also on its emotional, historical, future, or relational worth.

Sometimes that '68 Chevelle Malibu is worth bidding on because it's ridiculously priced and I know I could figure out something to do with it if I could get it for $1,200. Maybe I'll keep it, maybe I'll sell it, maybe I'll take a year to figure it out, but it's so dang cheap, I'm bidding.

Sometimes that '68 Chevelle Malibu is worth bidding on — no matter the price —because it was my first car. I want one, now that I'm forty, as a project car, and I can afford to spend pretty much anything I want to make my dream come true. I am not bidding based on my perception of its value as a commodity. I'm bidding based on the fact that it is a "treasure" to me.

Of course, real enthusiasts in any category can wear both hats at the same time. As the auctioneer, one of the most important discoveries you can make is that people can be involved for very different reasons. You can speak to those reasons and encourage their involvement.

There is an alternate way of looking at the bargain hunter versus treasure hunter metaphor. Economists refer to two types of valuations that inform bidders on how much to bid:

Interdependent Value: (Or as I call it, public value). Here are a few examples:

- It's common knowledge that a pair of True Religion Jeans cost around $200. You can buy them in various places, and if you're trying to auction them, then the value of your goods (in people's minds) are going to be governed and influenced by these interdependent bits of information.

- If you are selling custom-made knives, and it's common knowledge that your knives always sell for $500 or more, and you're the only source because you're an artisan knife maker, then that's going to shape the bidders' perceptions of the item's worth.

Private Value: This is the other type of valuation, which I call personal value. Here are a couple of examples:

- If you're a dad, and you feel guilty that you're never home, and your daughter asks for something special she saw on eBay, then the valuation is a private matter. It's not about the cost of the materials or how long it took to make. It's not about how much the dad has in his toy budget. It's about the dad's relationship to his daughter and his emotional state of mind.

- If you grew up on Broadway Street, and you see that exact street sign for sale on eBay, then your valuation is completely personal, and may not seem rational to anyone else.

Let me ask you something. Why would anyone pay $100 for a pair of 18-inch doll jeans that were made from chopped-up True Religion Jeans? (That question has crossed my mind a lot over the last few years.) That was the first $100 sale we made at Liberty Jane. Crazy, right? Maybe that buyer loves True Religion, loves their American Girl doll, and wants to have a shared experience — and spending $100 to make that a reality seems reasonable.

As an auctioneer, what's important is to suspend judgment, not make assumptions, and realize you won't ever know what people are thinking unless you have the good fortune of sitting down and chatting with the bidder over a nice dinner and hearing their story.

Imagine, for example, the winning bidder of an $100 Liberty Jane outfit is:

- a dad, sitting next to his seven-year-old daughter at the children's hospital as she undergoes chemotherapy. Her doll is the most important thing to her as she battles this horrible disease, and she has asked for a special outfit for her doll. He looks on eBay on his laptop and sees one called "Santa Cruz Bonfire" and remembers that the most fun he and his daughter ever had was at Santa Cruz last summer. Private value, right?

- a billionaire mom has her daughter's birthday wish list in front of her, and all it says is "Liberty Jane Jeans for Chrissa" (that's the American Girl doll's name). Private value, right?
- a collector who has watched every auction you've ever done, knows the prices your items go for, and is bidding because she knows the item is currently valued below what it should be. Public value, right?

As the auctioneer, it's important to consider how you can encourage each type of bidder. How?

Speak to private value bidders by using phrases like these in your listings:

- "This would make a great gift."
- "You deserve one special outfit."
- "You'll be able to pass this on to your grandchildren."
- "Your daughter will love this."
- "This will be a treasured keepsake."

Speak to public value bidders by using these kinds of words and phrases in your listings:

- Rare
- Collectible
- Numbered tags
- Limited Edition

- This item regularly sells for $100.

- The Kelly Blue Book (or other industry standard) value is X.

It's important to realize this isn't simply addressing emotional versus factual concerns. It's about understanding what motivates your bidders and encouraging those motives with positive messages and clear descriptions. Since you have no way of knowing their motives, it's best to add information in your listings that speaks to both of these scenarios.

Buyer Comfort

Have you ever been asked to play a game with your cousins after Thanksgiving dinner? They pull out some game they love, but guess what? You've never heard of it before. All of a sudden, you realize that the next few hours are going to be a bummer.

Your only strategy, other than politely declining to play, is to play several times and lose, knowing that over time you will gain the experiences needed to win, right? But even then, you know you will have to lose for several games, or hands, or rounds, or whatever. It won't be fun.

Have you been in this same situation where money is on the line? Big money? Imagine walking into a casino and sitting down at a game you aren't familiar with and plunking down a thousand bucks.

If you don't clarify the rules and explain what you're doing on eBay, then you're putting your bidders in exactly this same situation.

I'm sure there are many more, but here are a few "Seller Rules" that you should always add to the game, so your bidders quickly become comfortable. Quick comfort is the name of the game. The more you clarify the rules, the better your chances of having a pleasing final bid price. What should you clarify?

- Transparency: the clear facts and figures about the item (represented in both words and pictures)
- Availability: the true scarcity versus the abundance of the item, its condition, and what they get
- Credibility: as a seller specifically, who are you? Are a lot of people happy with you?
- Social Proof: indications of the item's worth, including external valuations, perspectives on the item, or third party endorsements.

In addition to these subliminal rules, you should also have explicit selling rules, like your shipping time, return policy, guarantee, etc. These add meaning, too, by conveying to the bidders that you are a professional.

The comfort level of your bidders radically influences their bidding behavior. This is such an enormous part of having a successful auction, yet most sellers don't think about it very much at all.

High Comfort = Bold Bidder Action

When a bidder has a high degree of comfort with what is going on, they become bold bidders. The opposite is true, as well. As their uncertainty grows, their boldness declines.

People also want to know as much as possible about what is going on as the auction unfolds. Feeding your bidders information and making them comfortable is the single greatest element for success in auctioneering. Violating this basic rule will take tens, hundreds, and even thousands of dollars off the table.

This is common sense when you think about it. The comfort level of each participant with the rules of the game and the reality of what is happening radically influences their behavior. If people have unanswered questions or "red flags" about even the smallest of details, they temporarily put those concerns out of their heads if their desire for the object outweighs their concerns. But as the stakes of an auction get higher and higher, those red flags re-emerge as buzz kills. They become the showstoppers that turn an active bidder into a watcher.

The tools involved in creating comfort are not mysteries:

- Clear facts about the item
- Clear, high-quality pictures
- Details about who you are (people buy from people)
- Your credibility indicators
- Social proof that the item is valuable
- Credible third-party endorsements
- A very low starting bid price
- Details about the scarcity versus abundance of the item. Is it one-of-a-kind? Or will you sell another one tomorrow?

Here is the critical lesson in regard to rule #1: eBay has set up a lot of the rules for the auction system and people generally know these eBay rules.

But as the auctioneer, you also set up a whole collection of your own rules. If you set them up well, people get comfortable. Set them up poorly or leave them unstated, and people get uncomfortable. The clearer you make your rules, the more comfort the seller will have. If you fail to set up your rules clearly, or don't set them up at all, your bidders will have a serious comfort problem. This is a huge mistake.

"The only thing we have to fear is fear itself — nameless, unreasoning, unjustified terror which paralyzes needed efforts to

convert retreat into advance."

This is one famous quote from the late president Franklin D. Roosevelt on his First Inaugural Address on March 4, 1933.

It's true for auctions, too — fear immobilizes people. And if they won't act because they are afraid of your deal, then you won't have a successful auction. Comfort reduces fear.

Make people comfortable!

Factor Six: Rival Vs. Non-Rival Goods

"A competitor will find a way to win. Competitors take bad breaks and use them to drive themselves just that much harder. Quitters take bad breaks and use them as reasons to give up. It's all a matter of pride."

– Nancy Lopez

There is a big difference between rival and non-rival goods. Understanding how a 'custom' item impacts the sales price is important for eBay sellers. Picasso was a seller of handmade items.

The story of his selling strategy is both interesting and instructive. He was a busy guy and, according to Wikipedia, his life's work included the following: 1,885 paintings, 1,228 sculptures, 2,880 ceramics, roughly 12,000 drawings, many thousands of prints, and numerous tapestries and rugs.

Picasso was well known for keeping his artwork "off the market" as much as possible to ensure that there was a sense of scarcity — and he used auctions (held through his network of fans and patrons in places like New York) to help establish his premium pricing.

He was acutely aware that his work was valued not based on the time involved, or the ink, or materials used, but on the intangible quality of his brand's power in the international marketplace. He knew what his pieces sold for at auction, and he took that as a basis for justifying premium prices.

If you are making handmade goods, then you are selling rival goods, too, like Picasso. We aren't Apple. We aren't Hasbro or Nike. We aren't mass manufacturers. We are more like Picasso (maybe not in terms of skill, but at least in terms of what we're doing). And if we price our items at the same price point as mass-manufactured items, we are making a huge mistake.

When it comes to pricing your items, there is one exceptional concept that governs this whole idea. Economists call it rival versus non-rival goods. It sounds fancy, but it's really pretty simple.

A rival good is one that people have to fight over if they want it, because there is a limited supply (a rivalry occurs). Examples include:

- the Hope Diamond
- a Picasso painting
- 12 slices of pizza sitting in front of a hungry football team

When a rival good is up for auction and it has a strong perceived value in people's minds, people fight, prices escalate, winners win, and losers lose. People immediately recognize that scarcity will create competition for the item.

A non-rival good is one that has infinite supply. Examples include:

- Liberty Jane digitally downloaded patterns
- iTunes songs
- broadcast TV

Any digitally delivered product falls into this category unless someone is artificially controlling supply. When you're shopping for a non-rival good, there is no need to rush; there is enough for everyone because there is an endless supply. There is no rivalry amongst the buyers. If you want it, you buy it, and there is still an infinite number of "copies" available for the next person.

Mass manufacturing has blurred the lines between these two ideas. There are a finite number of iPhones; it is a rival good, but Apple has made so many, it can act like the phones are a non-rival good when deciding on pricing. This is pretty much true for any mass-manufactured item. Companies sometimes manipulate this deliberately by making a finite number of each design, then escalating the price and creating perceived scarcity (think Porsche). But for most mass-manufactured items, there are plenty of copies available.

Fixed Prices vs. Auctions

Fixed prices are appropriate for non-rival goods because there are enough for everyone, there is no need to fight, and no opportunity for sellers to profit from the rivalry.

In addition to companies manipulating this deliberately, occasionally this system of non-rival, fixed pricing breaks down. We realize this when a product is so popular that it outpaces manufacturing. When Apple releases a cool new product and only makes 3 million, and a lot of people want one, what happens? You see the product on eBay selling for crazy prices because some smart marketer has identified the fact that with a shortage of supply, there is an opportunity to get higher prices.

On the other hand, auctions are appropriate for rival goods because there are not enough for everyone, and there is an opportunity to profit from the rivalry. As a seller of rival goods, your best selling strategy is an auction format if you have a good product and can attract a crowd. Why? Because you acknowledge that there are more people who want the item than there are items, and the only fair way to settle it is through an auction.

The best selling strategy for a non-rival good is a fixed price, because there is no concern in anyone's mind about scarcity. You just set a reasonable price and let the market decide about the popularity. If it's not popular, you end up discounting until people see it as a good value.

If you have a rival good and your selling strategy is to act like it's a non-rival good, then you're failing to use rivalry when you legitimately should.

If you're making 18-inch doll clothes, then think about this: Are you pricing your items at the same level as American Girl? The brand has an almost infinite supply; you only have a few. Shouldn't you take advantage of this scarcity? If you price your products the same as the Chinese imports and try to sell it in the same way (with a fixed, buy-it-now pricing strategy), then you're making a massive mistake.

This concept of rival goods is why we so strongly recommend the auction format for artisans. Picasso's strategy makes a lot of sense when you have both a rival good and an auction format opportunity, such as eBay.

Here is the bottom line: If you can make your product well and attract a following, then you should price it like Picasso via a two-step process. First, use auctions to help create a sense of rivalry and competition, and then use that brand credibility to establish your premium prices. That's been our approach at Liberty Jane, and it works. As our partners have implemented this approach, it has worked for them, too.

Manage the rivalry. Don't lie about anything — you don't have to — just be honest. You can only make a limited number of handmade, hand-carved, or hand-painted items in your home or studio. You're not a Chinese factory. Make people realize that — and get paid what you're worth! Price it like Picasso!

Manage Information Wisely

You can inadvertently share information that will damage the auction's final result. You've got to watch out for that, too. I don't mean just obvious information like, "this item is broken." I mean more subtle messages. Let's look at some examples.

Suppose you're auctioning a limited edition set of hand-carved knives, and you have four sets. Consider the impact of this phrase in your auction listing:

"I never extend second chance offers." (A second chance offer allows the bidder in the second position to get one of the products for the amount of money they offered, in essence a discount on the top bidder's price).

What is this saying to bidders? It's telling the second place bidder that if they really want the item, the only way it's going to happen is if they increase their bid to the top spot.

Now consider the impact of this statement:

"Second chance offers will be considered if the auction exceeds my expected price."

What are you saying to the bidders? You're telling them that second place is the most financially prudent spot to take if your secret pricing conditions are met. What's the problem with this? Obviously, if you have financially motivated buyers and everyone wants to be in second place, you're not going to see your bid prices rise aggressively as everyone waits for someone else to take the top spot. It's confusing the situation. Bad move.

What if you don't say anything about second chance offers, but then after the auction is over, you offer the second place bidder the item for their final bid price, which is less than the winning bidder paid.

You've just sold two items for almost an identical price, but only paid the listing fees for one of the items. Good for you, right?

But what message are you sending to the second place bidder? On face value, you're saying, "Hurray for you, you get one of the items, too!" But you're also telling them by your actions that you don't have to be the winner to be a winner. Who cares? Well, if you are a regular seller and this buyer is a regular customer of your auctions, you've just planted a very bad thought in their mind —*I can be in the game, but not push for the top spot, and I'll probably still get what I want*. In an auction environment, this is a very bad message to give a bidder. Manage information wisely if you want to maximize final bid prices!

The Downside of Using Fixed Prices for Rival Goods

We advocate a two-step selling system: auctions to establish your premium position in the market, then high-priced, buy-it-now items supported by the auction results. However, there are real forces that work to undermine and erode your premium pricing.

You have to be willing to fight the forces that will try to suppress your pricing power. You have to be willing to stand your ground. This is not about earnings as much as it is about your mindset and a determined point of view. As Malcolm X once said,

> "Nobody can give you freedom. Nobody can give you equality or justice or anything. If you're a man, you take it."

If you'll allow us to adapt this to pricing, we might say:

> "Nobody wants to pay a premium price, or pay what things are worth, or what you're asking. It's your job to make them."

So here are the forces you have to learn to fight against:

Anchoring: Anchoring is a complicated psychological concept. When you boil it all down, it means that people cannot forget about relevant (and even irrelevant) numbers and prices related to your offer. Those numbers and prices will affect their decisions. For 18-inch doll clothes, it is the American Girl (AG) catalog, and it's those prices that are drilled into everyone's minds. You cannot price higher than AG without overcoming several challenges. Their prices are an anchor.

Even though we've tried to cultivate a "high-end" and "exclusive" brand (generally people have chosen to affirm that), it was hard to get away from the AG anchor. The best way to do it is through an auction, where over time the anchor becomes your average selling price, rather than the comparison to the marketplace or market leader. In other words, people become focused on your previous sale prices more than they do other factors. But if you sell items at fixed prices, then you are tied to the market leader's anchor with no hope of avoiding it. People look at your price, then look at the AG catalog, then back at your price, and they either say, "Yep, this makes sense," or "Nah, I don't think so."

The anchor can also work against you in another way. If you sell buy-it-now items and then try to do an auction at the same time, why would anyone ever bid an amount higher than the buy-it-now price you've advertised on your site somewhere else — even if it's for a slightly different outfit? They wouldn't. It's an anchor. Bad move. So anchors have to be used to help you and not hurt you.

The good news for you is that there are appropriate high-priced anchors that you can reference and use as points of comparisons as you create your listings. Our auctions at Liberty Jane are one anchor in the doll clothing space and there are others that are even better than ours.

So, if I were writing your item description for you, I might say something like, "We are inspired by the quality and intense craftsmanship of [insert top seller's name] and aspire to be like them." This gives your bidder a point of reference (an anchor) based on a high price point of the other seller while still being totally respectful and kind to the other seller.

See how this works? You just can't say, "We are better than [insert seller name]" and expect to get a higher price by making that claim.

Earnings: If you're going to make a custom item, why sell it for $19 when you can auction it and (if you do our auction system steps) possibly get a lot more? The math works better via auctions. That's the bottom line.

Yeah, there is a risk of having it go for less, but if you are making a good product, taking good pictures, and following our auction system steps, then you're going to be better off doing an auction. But if you're short-sighted and desperately need money, then you'll feel the pressure to start selling things for buy-it-now prices without first establishing your ultra-premium brand reputation. Your need for money will tempt you to start lowering your prices.

Complaints: Our biggest issue with selling fixed-price items in the doll clothes category is that the American Girl anchor (their price points) hypnotize people, so if you try to list an item higher than that, customers constantly have one request: "Lower your prices." What are they saying? They're saying, "Hey, in my head, I have a number, and yours is too much higher than that number, so I'm unhappy with you."

This is a total buzz kill, and unfortunately people often make these "lower your prices" comments in public places, almost as a way to scold you for trying to go "up market" and be an ultra-premium provider. So you're compelled to argue or defend your prices. It's a hassle. It's horrible. If you had a private counter at Neiman Marcus, then you could get away with high fixed-priced items, because no one would shout, "Lower your prices!" But this isn't Neiman Marcus; this is the Internet.

Our selling system — which involves holding auctions to establish ultra-premium prices, then selling fixed-price items on your own website — is designed to side-step complaining. How? Consider these benefits of our system. In an auction:

1. We aren't setting the price; the crowd is in charge of that.

2. No one can complain and tell us to lower our auction prices.

3. In an auction, no one seems to care about the AG anchor, because we make sure our prior sales are well publicized as a relevant anchor.

4. The final bid price of your outfit sets the stage for your next auction. The last auction's ending price is frequently the new floor.

5. When your auction ends high, it validates your "custom" or" "VIP" buy-it-now pricing. Why would anyone expect you to make a custom outfit and sell it for $30 when your outfits sell at auction for over $300?

People will pay what other people paid

Re-read that sentence slowly and let me unpack it. People (meaning the newly arriving crowd) will pay what other people (the happily leaving crowd) have paid. As the new bidders enter the scene and see (and believe) that the previous customers had a nice experience at the $75 price point, they'll follow in their footsteps and pay that same price.

Here is an example (which I'm sure you can relate to at any price point):

Have you ever walked into a restaurant that is fancier than where you would normally eat? It's full of people, and as you look at the prices on the menu, you think, *What?* But then you calm down, look around the restaurant, and see all the happy people happily ordering and think, *Okay, I guess this is how it works here — and it's worth it.* You ponder all the good things that will happen if you maintain your composure. You stay calm because, after all, you don't want to look cheap. You just decide to go along with it all. Sometimes the shock is too great, or your wallet is too empty, and you do have to get up and leave. But much more frequently, you decide to stay. If the restaurant delivers great service, you're probably going to remember a very pleasant experience that you would even like to repeat someday.

That's social proof in action, and fostering it in your eBay auctions is a huge part of getting high final bid prices. You are in exactly the same situation as the restaurant owner, except you probably have no overhead costs to worry about, no employees to pay, and no food spoiling in the kitchen. The beauty of the Internet is that if you get it wrong today, you can try again tomorrow with a different approach. Deliver a great experience. Let people remember their interactions with you as something they would like to repeat.

The Downside of Social Proof

Let's look at the reverse: Do people regularly pay you nothing for your item by not bidding? Remember, people will pay what other people paid, so you've got a real problem if this is happening. Keep reading to learn about solving this problem with spiral management.

If people come to your auction and see no bids, then they look at your other items for sale and see no bids, and they look at your transaction history and see a lot of no bidding. . . Guess what they're going to do — NOT BID!

Your failure today will reinforce your failure tomorrow unless you make some changes. Someone once said,

"The definition of insanity is doing the same thing and expecting a different outcome."

What will people pay for something? It's anyone's guess, right? You know the price you want to get, and sometimes you're tempted to put your products out as a buy-it-now items with this "ideal price" plugged right in for the whole world to see. You think that by telling people what the price should be, they will agree. You figure you'll just tell everyone what you think your items are worth and require them to agree with you.

However, given the way eBay is structured, if your item ends and no one has validated your price point by saying "yes" and buying the item, then your failure is public and it damages your credibility.

Every time you fail publicly at a certain price point, you are training your bidders to expect lower prices next time. But bidders or buyers don't value your opinion about price. Do you care what the used car salesman says about what a car is worth? No way! You only care what the wisdom of the crowd, or a third-party authority, says that it's worth.

Your Opening Bid Price

Sellers using eBay should seriously consider the psychological impact of using a low opening bid price and having no reserve price. It's the best approach almost all the time. Follow me on this:

If you have a high opening bid and/or reserve price, what you're saying to the bidder (or prospective bidder) is:

1. I don't trust you guys to value this properly, and I want to protect myself from your stupidity.

2. I don't trust eBay to deliver the participants necessary to make this auction work, and I want to protect myself from their incompetence.

3. I want to be the "winner," or I won't actually let this play out.

Is any of that comforting to the bidder? Does any of that sound like it will produce a good customer experience? No. And bidders know that. Even if they haven't stopped to think about it in such clear terms, they know it in their gut. And uncomfortable bidders are not bold bidders.

Remember that your pricing strategy is a reflection of your brand strategy. Price wisely.

Factor Seven: Popularity, Novelty, Scarcity

"To my mind the old masters are not art; their value is in their scarcity."

– Thomas Edison

There is a big difference between popularity, novelty, and scarcity. In the end, scarcity is the most important thing to manage.

Popularity: The popularity of an item is important; I grant you that. The more people there are who want something, the higher its price will go — that's basic supply and demand. If you are fortunate enough to have created something popular, congratulations, but there are two serious problems with just focusing on popularity. Here they are:

- What if there are only two people who want something and their names are Bill Gates and Warren Buffet? As the auctioneer, do you care if no one else is interested? Do you care if the item is popular? Do you think the auction will do well? You don't need popularity to be successful.

- In almost all cases, if something is popular, manufacturers in China (or elsewhere) will have figured out how to flood the market with a reasonable substitute. Those imitations will dilute the demand for the product significantly. No popular artisan item stays unmanufactured for very long (which is why it it so critical to develop your brand).

Novelty: Is novelty important for creating the perception of worth and generating bidding action? Sure. There are good reasons why the Hard Rock Café displays guitars played by rock legends like Jimi Hendrix. That stuff is interesting to look at and talk about. Lots of people enjoy having something unique and special. A sense of novelty in your product creation is certainly helpful.

Selling novelties is easy. A penny that was mis-stamped, a stuffed three-headed alligator, a pair of 501 jeans worn by James Dean, a small ghost town in Eastern Washington. People love to have something to talk about, show people, obsess over, and enjoy.

The problem with novelty is that many times, it's very difficult to get people to pay the premium price for the authentic item if there are reasonable substitutes available. If you're in the market for a three-headed alligator, is it really worth the added $4,000 you'll have to pay to get a real one, compared to the $19 you can pay for a fake? If you're the auctioneer, novelty doesn't usually pay the rent.

Scarcity: If there is one single piece of information that dictates bid action more than anything else and makes bidders get into a good old-fashioned showdown, it is the scarcity of the item. Scarcity fuels bidder competition like nothing else. Your job as the auctioneer is to manage the scarcity (or perceived scarcity) very carefully.

Perceived Scarcity Radically Impacts Bidder Decisions

If you're the maker of handcrafted goods, then like Picasso, you are responsible for managing the availability of your inventory. If you flood the market, you're not going to do well. Control distribution very closely, and you'll have a better chance of doing well.

Here are five ways to manage scarcity:

1. Use limited edition sets. Make your products or outfits (if you're sewing clothes) as limited edition sets. This creates a built- in mechanism to explain and clarify the rarity of the items.

2. Frequently come up with vibrant and bold names and designs. There is nothing better than having a new and amazing design to create buzz, and then limiting production to just 10 total copies.

3. Don't sell all your limited edition copies at one time; trot them out one at a time slowly, and make each auction special.

4. Be comfortable "going dark." Having nothing in your store is fine if people realize you have times or seasons for selling, as well as times and seasons for creating. For us, it is simple — we try to copy the fashion industry and produce a "Fall Line" and a "Spring Line." This allows us to manage people's expectations very clearly.

5. Be willing to "pull it off the market" for sale at a later date. If you have a limited edition set that is not getting a good final bid price, simply stop listing that item. Take the remainder and save it for a later date. Bring it back closer to Christmas or even a year or two later when you're customers are better trained.

Factor Eight: Reputation

"You can't build a reputation on what you are going to do."

– Henry Ford

The most important question to ask when it comes to reputation is: Are your items selling for a high price compared to the competition? This is the single most important issue when it comes to reputation.

You've got to get a positive selling experience happening. It's a virtuous spiral. When you get a virtuous spiral going, it sets the stage for you to either:

1. Do it again.

2. Do something similar, because you've proven your success through the first effort.

Here is an example:

You launch your eBay efforts with a nice outfit, (if you're selling doll clothes), you have 12 bidders, and the outfit goes for $39 (the highest price you've ever achieved). Now, when you do another auction, you'll have this positive event working for you in several ways:

1. New people who don't know about you will come in and look at your selling history. They'll see that prior sale price and realize that other people value your items. They'll respect you for that. If they like the item, they will jump into the bidding.

2. People who participated in the first auction will see that if they want your stuff, they are going to have to compete for it.

3. Auction winners who are happy with your products will likely want more and become loyal customers.

4. Happy buyers will leave positive feedback and, in that way, signal to everyone watching that the price they paid was well worth it.

If you get this working, then you're off to the races as your virtuous spiral begins to build from one success to the next. What's important at this point is to keep the process working, listen to the customers, and tweak things to maximize your success, and then just rinse and repeat. If you're a frequent seller and you've developed a following, then the way your auctions end will frequently determine the way the next one will begin.

Here are my tips for starting a virtuous spiral:

1. Sell your items in limited editions, or other well-conceived "scarce" methods. Tell everyone the details. Are you making five of this item and no more? Be clear about the scarcity of your item in the listing.

2. Do everything you can to stand out, including (and most importantly) communicating that you have something very special to sell, as well as using terrific photography to capture the quality of the item.

3. Become very consistent with your auction start dates and end dates so people know what's going on. Train people as to your process and methods. For example, always list your items on Sunday at 6pm Pacific. Always launch your auctions on the first Sunday in June and first Sunday in November (or whatever your preferred schedule is).

4. Upgrade your photography.

5. Upgrade your listing descriptions including the guarantee, testimonials, and embedded content.

6. Do a newsletter and always highlight your current items up for auction. Make sure you clarify the deal, such as how many you're doing, why these are special, what they've sold for previously, etc. Send your newsletter out four or five hours before your auction ends for maximum impact. If you're not sure how to do email marketing, pick up a copy of our e-book *Email Marketing Power*.

7. Start building more ways to draw a crowd into your auctions (a Facebook fan page, blog subscriptions, additional newsletters, etc.).

8. Become very good at getting and using testimonials. The power of a testimonial is huge. It's called a third-party endorsement. If you say your stuff is great, people will be skeptical; but if a raving fan says the same thing, it carries more credibility.

One of the best things you can do for your auction business is to start a virtuous spiral. It is a self-reinforcing positive feedback loop. The opposite of this principle is true, as well. You need to stop failing. Failing in an auction business is a negative reinforcing feedback loop.

A negative feedback loop, also known as a vicious spiral or death spiral, is when you fail and that failure sets the stage for ongoing failure.

The easiest example is having an auction that flops. It happens to everybody. It can shake your confidence so badly that you vow to leave the auction business completely. We know; we've had one that we still remember in horror and talk about with disgust. It was a beautiful outfit that took four or five hours to make, and we spent at least an hour taking pictures and making the listing. It sold for $8. Wow, we were so mad. Simply in terms of time and effort, it needed to sell for $50 to $60. And that had been our average auction price at that point, so we knew it could happen. It is super frustrating when you fail that badly.

In addition to the fact that we only made $8 for all the hours of hard work, we also realized that this failure sent a lot of bad messages, including:

- Our prior buyers who paid more than $8 saw this result, they are now thinking they overpaid.
- Based on this result, anyone who likes to compare thinks that our stuff is less valuable than the low quality, imported stuff.
- If new bidders come along to our next auction and they see this result in our seller history, then they'll think, *Hey, I can probably get one of their outfits at the $8 price, so I'll pass on bidding for this one that has a $78 current bid price.*

All bad messages! Have you had this happen to you before? You're not alone.

Here is my advice for how to stop a death spiral:

1. Stop your listings for a week or two. Just stop. This helps with scarcity.
2. Consider how you're managing scarcity. Are you doing limited edition sets? Are your outfits or items just too available?
3. Find successful examples in your category and look at their listings (don't even focus on the quality of their actual item compared to yours). Just look at the presentation.

    a. Are their pictures better?

    b. Are their descriptions longer?

    c. Is their guarantee clearer?

    d. Are there testimonials included in their descriptions?

    e. Do they use eBay's "listing designer" and have a nice listing border?

    f. Do they have embedded photos or videos?

    g. Are they listing their items to end at a different time?

4. Figure out what they're doing differently and prepare to copy their presentation method. Copy what works. This is no different than what everyone in business (and even non-profit work) does. If the church across town gets a huge jumbo screen, your pastor is going to want one. If Safeway starts offering a coupon program, Walgreens is going to want to launch one. That's just being contemporary. Obviously, because of color schemes, photography, word choices, and graphics, your final listing really can be uniquely yours. Ideally, it won't look like anyone else's; it will just have the same tone and professionalism. And I'm not recommending you copy someone's listing. We've had people do that to us, and it's really frustrating. If you complete the steps outlined in this book, it will be the case that people copy you, not the other way around. You'll have to deal with the imitators, and although that can be frustrating, it is (in some ways) a compliment.

5. Review the quality of your item compared to your category competitors. Are you as good as them? Can you be? Be brutally honest with yourself, but don't take it personally. Maybe you're just not as good and you need to lower your expectations for success. Or, maybe you are as good, but you realize your photography has been killing your success. If you can upgrade your actual craftsmanship, do it.

6. Plan your re-launch, including when your auction is going to end (shoot for Sunday night) and how you're going to get the word out — Facebook? Email? A newsletter?

7. Launch and then do whatever you can to get people informed and involved.

How to Build Credibility

As an eBay seller, your credibility matters tremendously. As a credible seller, people will pay to work with you. Here are seven ways to increase your credibility. There are lots more, but this is a pretty good list:

1. Create an eBay store. It makes you look more established than a non-store owner. Yeah, you'll have to pay for this service, but it may very well be worth it.

2. Have a robust "about me" page.

3. Reach PowerSeller status if you can (but don't give away the farm to get it). We had PowerSeller status, and we decided that the volume of selling on eBay necessary to keep it wasn't wise for us. But if you can sell enough to keep the status, you should.

4. Strive for Top Rated Seller status.

5. Send emails to your eBay mailing list (and any other mailing lists) and discuss the prices you're getting for your items. It's not bragging if you word it properly, and it sends a very important message — it tells everyone how other people are treating you and your goods.

6. Produce stunning photography. Amateurs take bad pictures with bad cameras. Don't do that!

7. Re-quote your best customer feedback often and in lots of places.

8. Set up a blog or other non-eBay venue where people can read more, see more, and learn more. You are allowed to have a link to sites like this in your "about me" page.

9. Compose a user ID that means something, looks well thought out, and implies credibility. Have a bad user ID? Yes, you can change it.

12 Ways To Increase Credibility

Brendon Burchard, the founder of the "Experts Academy," lists 12 ways you can increase your credibility, including:

1. Insights and perspectives — share them with people.
2. Philosophy — have an interesting point of view.
3. Personal path or testimony — share it.
4. Formal position or experience — it counts.
5. Popularity — are people liking your work? Share it.
6. Partnerships — are you partnering with someone credible?
7. Progress — can you reference your progress?
8. Praise — what are people saying? Quote them.
9. Press or performances — are you "on stage"? Let people know about it.
10. Paying clients — Have VIP clients? Let people know.
11. Promotions— Have you been featured on a popular site? Share it.
12. Products — do you have something exciting to sell?

Factor Nine: Giant Crowds

"With the crowds on your side, it's easier to play up to your potential."

– Julius Erving

If you're making a good product and taking good photos, then the single most important factor governing your success is probably the number of visitors to your auctions.

We've tracked this for our auctions in 2011 and 2012, and the findings were interesting. It is clear to us that the more visitors we have to an auction, the higher our prices go. Here is proof:

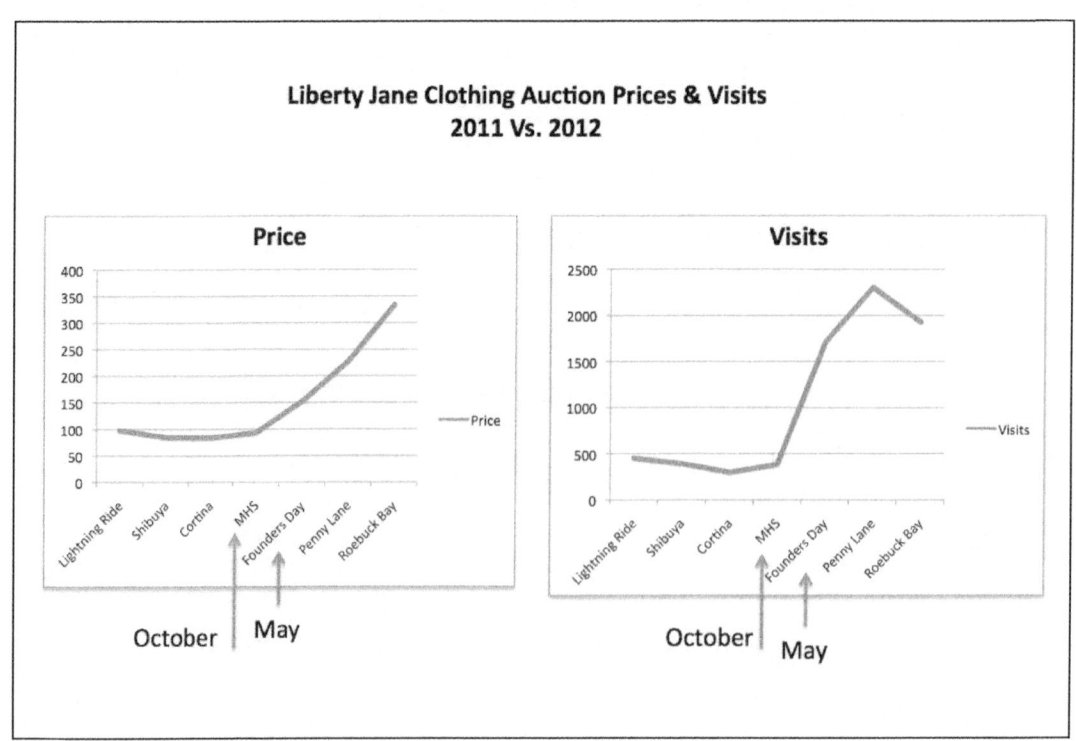

The auctions items are listed from left to right. The left chart shows the prices, and the right chart shows the number of visitors that came to the auctions. Notice the correlation.

There are steps you can take to draw a bigger crowd than you'll normally receive if you leave it all up to eBay (and our strong recommendation is that you don't leave it all up to eBay). The site can provide a good amount of traffic, but not enough to ensure you get exceptional prices.

Here are some important actions you should take to draw as many people into the crowd as possible:

For eBay auctions:

1. Find the right time for your auctions to end. Usually Sunday evening is considered the best eBay traffic time. But some categories are different; you've got to test things to see what's best for your category.

2. Be very consistent about when your auctions start and end. For example, our auctions always end on Sunday night. Telegraphing your punches is very helpful to people.

3. Have your newest auction start a few hours before your current auction ends. In that way, the maximum traffic brought in for the "dramatic conclusion" of one auction will see the next cool thing. And guess what? They're going to want to watch, bid, and win. It's like your auctions are a soap opera — the drama never stops.

4. If you're an eBay storeowner, send your eBay newsletters out four or five hours before your most important auction ends. That way, all your fans are prompted just in time to participate.

5. In your newsletter, when you feature an item, ensure you show a listing that has a high number of bids on it to

demonstrate to people that you have exciting things going on.

6. Consider paying for a premium or higher visibility listing on eBay.

For non-eBay auctions:

1. Tell people in all the appropriate places what you're going to sell. Include your blog, Facebook, eBay newsletter, Craigslist, message boards, or any other place you can find.

2. Cultivating your own email list is by far the very best way to get targeted traffic to your auctions. When we started in 2008, we had no email addresses. By the fall of 2009, we had 125. Today, we have almost 54,000. Trust me —when you have an auction running on eBay and you send an enthusiastic email out to 54,000 people, good things happen. To learn more about how we built our email list to this size, pick up a copy of our e-book *Email Marketing Power*.

3. Participate in and grow your following in the forums, or old-style message boards, where your target buyers hang out.

4. Create a Facebook fan page and, if you can afford it, advertise to find fans. Put auction updates with details about the auction in your Facebook updates. Do this a few hours before your auctions end.

5. After the auction ends, post a Facebook message that says, "Thanks everyone for making our auction a success — the final bid price was X" and show the result of the auction.

6. Develop a solid YouTube channel with some video content that is helpful to buyers and build your subscriber list there. Send them messages or make advertisement type videos and publish them prior to your auctions ending. Pick up a copy of *Youtube Marketing Power*.

7. Develop a Pinterest profile and cultivate a group of followers who will be included to participate in your auctions. Learn how we developed our Pinterest profile, pick up a copy of *Pinterest Power*.

8. Develop an Instagram profile and grow it. To learn how we are using Instagram, pick up a copy of *Instagram Power*.

The Six Participants in Any Competitive Auction

There are six roles that people will step into for a competitive auction. You should consider how to attract and work with each type of participant.

1. eBay: (How could we forget them?) They've made a lot of the rules, right? They are always there at everyone's auctions. Break their rules, and they'll become an active part of the drama.
2. You: (the auctioneer) You've made lots of the rules, too, and your actions are the most influential of all six participants.
3. The highest bidder: (At any given time, this person can change, but the behavior is constant regardless of which person is filling this spot.) This person gets a special treat at the end of the auction in addition to the item they've won; they get to know the other bidders' estimated value of the item. No one else gets to learn their estimates of the item's value; they get to keep that a secret. Economists call this "treat" the winner's curse. Because while they've won, they've also been educated to the fact that they've overestimated the item's worth to some degree compared to the rest of the participants. I don't see it as a curse however; I see it as a secret they get to keep.
4. The second place bidder: Sadly, this person loses out on the item and leaves the auction with nothing, unless you make a second chance offer to them. In that case, they leave in better shape than the winner, since they received the item for a discount on the final bid price. (Although, as previously stated, this has negative consequences as well).

5. The tertiary bidders: These include all the folks who have helped the bid price climb, but have stopped actively bidding at some point. However, they did push the final bid price along in incredibly important ways.
6. The crowd: (viewers) They are mesmerized, tempted to bid, and curious about how the item will end. They could at any moment jump in and take the high bidder spot. Maybe they are your competitors just checking it all out, maybe they're previous buyers, or maybe they are preparing to bid on your next auction.

While it's true that you only need two active bidders to make an auction escalate, the larger the crowd of honestly interested potential bidders, the more bid action you'll see and the higher final bid price you'll achieve.

Why is this always true? The single most important reason to have a crowd is going to sound like a cliché, but it's not. Here it is: There is safety in numbers.

As the auctioneer, you're nervously waiting to see how it's all going to play out, right? And if you've believed my "low opening bid" rant and you've set your opening bid price extremely low, you are taking a risk, right?

And the best way to mitigate that risk is to have a large number of people attend the event, and have them be armed with enough facts about your product to know when it's selling for too low a price. The wisdom of the crowd will help protect you.

Appendix A: Assessment Guide

You've got nine factors. Now it's time to put it all together. We've created a simple assessment guide. You can use it to judge your current auction work and identify the areas you need to improve.

A great way to create an objective perspective is to go find a successful seller in your category and use the assessment guide on one of their auctions. Then identify the areas where they are stronger than you and the areas where you're stronger than them. Use a Liberty Jane auction if you want. Be systematic and try to make improvements little by little.

An Auction System Assessment Guide

Factor/Score	1	2	3	4	5
Brand					
Design					
Craftsmanship					
Photography					
Writing					
Rivalry					
Scarcity					
Crowd Sourcing					

To help you use the assessment guide, we're suggesting you use these five ratings:

Rating Descriptions:

1 = Missing or counterproductive

2 = Marginally or infrequently used

3 = Average

4 = Well done, but not flawless

5 = Exceptionally done

Factor Descriptions:

Branding: Has the seller used all of the tools available to construct a brand that conveys deep meaning? Is it unique and memorable? Does the brand go beyond the obvious and convey something special about the seller's vision and intent?

Craftsmanship: Is the work done to exacting standards? Is it made from top-quality materials? Is there legitimate professionalism and excellence?

Design: Is the work scaled properly, well-conceived as a concept, proportionate, and surprising? Is the material choice supportive of the concept? Is it focused?

Photography: Are the photos professional? Are they sharp and in focus? Are the lighting and background appropriate? Do they flatter the garment?

Writing: Is the writing a thorough and well-constructed description of the outfit, the seller, the scarcity, and the social proof? Are there added elements like videos, extra pictures, and quotes that share detailed information? Is there adequate explanation of the seller's intentions? Is it fun to read?

Rivalry: Are pricing strategies structured for maximum success, including a low starting bid price and no reserve? Are second chance offers managed carefully and clearly expressed? Does buy-it-now pricing elsewhere in the store undermine auction success? Does the seller tell people what they should expect to pay?

Scarcity: Is the description very clear about the limited availability of the outfit? Does the description convey a sense of urgency and finite buying options? Is it clearly presented as a one-of-a-kind or a limited edition set?

Crowd Sourcing: Is the seller using every option available to identify and engage potential customers? Is there an impressive crowd showing up for the auctions? Are non-eBay or non-Etsy strategies in place and driving traffic?

Appendix B: Success Checklist

Here is a step-by-step check list in the form of questions that might be helpful in planning and executing your auctions:

- o Branding: Have I created a compelling brand for my work that conveys deep meaning?
- o Branding: Have I clarified my position in the market through my messages and selling results?
- o Design: Is my design compelling to a specific category of buyer (either trendy, historical, or some other specialty)?
- o Scarcity: Have I made a finite number of the items, clearly stated that they are going to be sold as a limited edition set?
- o Scarcity: Have I announced how quickly (or slowly) they'll be sold?
- o Craftsmanship: Does my finished product look professionally crafted? Do my pictures convey that nicely?
- o Photography: Are my pictures professional and impressive?
- o Writing: Are my descriptions robust and thorough, outlining all the details and answering a lot of questions?
- o Writing: Are the names of my products interesting and fun?
- o Writing: Does my description include "wow" factors (video, quotes, extra pictures)?
- o Pricing: Is my starting bid price set low?
- o Pricing: If using a buy-it-now strategy, have I justified the high price?

- o Crowd: Is my auction end date scheduled at a good time (Sunday night?), and am I being consistent with my auctions or sales so people know what to expect?

- o Crowd: Am I using off-site marketing strategies to drive traffic at the right time and to encourage participation in my auction or sale (like newsletters, Facebook sites, YouTube channels, Pinterest profiles, etc.)?

- o Reputation: Am I publicizing my results to let people know what my items are selling for?

- o Reputation: Am I adding extra elements in the packages I send to my buyers, like a personally written note card, or some other thank-you so the person will become a repeat customer?

Printed in Great Britain
by Amazon